For
Nicholas Lashmet
and
Jenny Peters
who survive the demigogues
of Arlington

and, too,
for
Anne Hamilton Hewitt Hislop
who has had the good fortune
never to drive through
Cleburne

Demons & Demigogues:
Political Fanaticism
In The Longhorn State

Arthur Frederick Ide

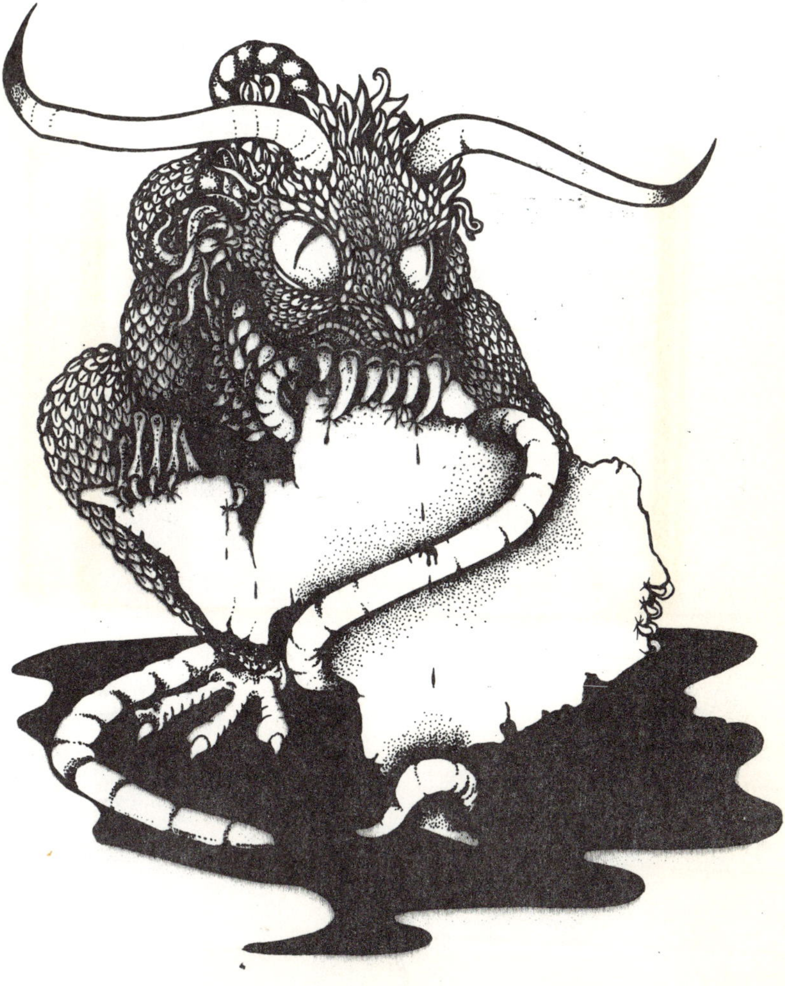

Las Colinas
Liberal Press
1985

Published by
The Liberal Press
P.O. Box 160361
Las Colinas, Texas 75016-9998

©1985, Arthur Frederick Ide

Library of Congress Cataloging-in-Publication Data
Ide, Arthur Frederick.
   Demons & demigogues.

   Bibliography: p.
   Includes index.
   1. Texas--Politics and government--1951-
2. Conservatism--Texas. 3. Politicians--Texas.
4. United States--Politics and government--1981-
I. Title. II. Title: Demons and demigogues.
F391.2.I33 1985   976.4'063   85-15879
ISBN 0-934659-00-1 (pbk.)

Table of Contents

Jan McKenna—Ayatollah of Arlington 1
Jim Norwood—To Be God or To Be Censor 7
Urban Pettiness & the Denial of Democracy 17
City of Garland 41
"Dr. No"—The Problem of Dick Armey 44
Ronald Reagan & Texas 56
David Stockman & America's Farmers 71
Ronald Reagan & Texas'
Radical Right Politicians 74
Terrorists in Texas 87
Neo-Nazism and the Legion of Doom 105
Kent Hance—Political Opportunist 116
Religious Fanaticism in Texas 123
The Old Guard: Democrat & Republican
and Yuppie Justice 144
Bill Ceverha—Taking Aim at:
Human Freedom 156
Index 165

Introduction

The *American Heritage* Dictionary has defined "fanaticism" as "excessive, irrational zeal," and a "fanatic" as a "person possessed by an excessive zeal for an uncritical attachment to a cause or position." Both words are derived from the Latin *fanaticus* which means "inspired by god." Texas has more than its share of "religious fanatics" whose fanaticism spills over like slurry onto the fertile ground of Texas bigotry, narrow-mindedness and overt orchestration to control the destinies of not only Texans but the world. Not only has this insanity been demonstrated by today's "Elmer Gantry"-style demigogues who take to tents or the ballrooms of popular motels—as illustrated on the following two pages (being a reproduction of a circular I found on my door one Wednesday afternoon, when returning home to Mesquite)—but in the chauvinistic choragus commencement of the Rev. Nathan Bickerstaff, 28, minister of a Waxahachie church who was arrested along with two other church members in May, for passing out religious literature in DeSoto by thrusting it into the cars of teenagers who were

READ WHAT GOD'S "PROPHET" SAYS

Emphasizes Repentance & Obedience To Truth

PREACHING AGAINST: Adultery, divorce & remarriage, marriage annulment, fornication, common-law living, oral sex, lusting, homosexuality, lesbianism, pimps, pornography, mixed bathing, women wearing shorts, hatred, stealing, cheating, lying, deceiving, gambling, using God's name in vain, dope addiction, alcoholic beverages, tobacco use, smoking, pride, make-up, certain television programs etc., suicide, murder, rape, bribery, extortion, arson, mini skirts, revenge, burglary, rock music, and all the rest that the Bible condemns!

Dear Folks,

Haven't you heard enough about the modern Seed-Faith, prosperity, health, and financial success at the expense of almost totally ignoring the basic teaching of Jesus such as repentance of sin which Christ emphasized and so did the prophet John the Baptist. Repentance means sorrow for one's sins and to be willing to forsake all deeds which the Bible condemns. They are listed on the front.

In many churches the pastors are afraid to point out sin because they are fearful of their congregation that they may be voted out, so he tends to please the people. The result is, more hypocrites in the pews, and yet they are boasting about their attendance.

If a person does not change their ways after claiming salvation, he or she is worse off than the publicized sinner. For now they are satisfied in the daily sins they commit.

Jesus said, you compass land and sea to make a prosylite and now he is ten times more a child of hell. In otherwords, you made him more wicked than he was before. Listen to what the prophet says and be ready for Jesus' coming. The blood of Jesus cleanses as you repent.

If you want to know what the Holy Ghost said concerning television sets, he said, "Move them out".

Love in Jesus name
"That Prophet"

"cruising the strip", to the blatantly bitter boisterousness of Paige Patterson who would squelch dissent in the Southern Baptist Convention by limiting all debate and centering all faith around the Christian bible which he believes is without error or internal contradiction.

These dangerous demigogues to human freedom are not satisfied in their rank proselytization for new converts to their staid and ossified way of thinking, but in their messages of hate psychologically coerce freedom loving individuals to rally against opposing opinions, different lifestyles and practices, and various other forms of what they determine to be "social deviance." The strangle hold of religion around the arteries of justice and objectivity have grown suffocatingly tight in bedroom communities near metropolitan areas, so that Cleburne carves out the heart of opportunity for the mentally handicapped, Mesquite menaces members of feminist groups who demand freedom of choice, a San Antonio City Councilwoman drapes her neronian attitude against a visable minority in a barbaric attempt to limit the Constitutional guarantee of freedom of assembly, and a Houston judge openly challenges the separation of church and state, surrendering taxpayers rights to a small coterie of psuedo-intellectuals, while the President of a state university collapses before the avalanche of political blackmail and publicly censors what adults might see—all in the name of what each calls "religion".

Continuing their attacks on dignity of being and liberty of conscience, these tyrants of today promise a greater purge and holocaust for Texans tomorrow. This book had to be written, even if it is but the only treatise against their promise of an impending dark age, a return to inquistorial inquiries, and the lawlessness not only of the old west which the legislator from Lake Jackson promises, but the mental, physical, and emotional enslavement that choked ideas and innovations in the Middle Ages. If this book is torched by one of these demigogues, it is the author's hope that the fire burns until light and justice can rule supreme once more in Texas.

—Arthur Frederick Ide
Mesquite, Texas

14 July 1985
Bastille Day

Jan McKenna
Ayatollah of Arlington

Ronald Reagan predicted that there will be a "second revolution" in America during his second term of office. He is right. But the revolution will be more than an economic riot. It will be a war with weapons—handguns which are becoming increasingly more common on the streets and in the rural areas of America. And they will be turned against citizens by both the military and by other civilians who feel threatened. The revolution will be bloody, and the streets and alleys will be red with civil war as individual greed becomes more popular than charity, civility, or the milk of human kindness. A growing gaggle of political geese and turkeys is appearing in most cities, where the enriched and limited few are aligning with the paranoid and troubled who would become gods, but settle to issue messages of hate and bigotry, radical racisim and redneck philosophy. These demigogue deities include local officials, such as Dallas City Councilman Jim Hart who called for

Jan McKenna

public lynchings of blacks in front of city government buildings "to set an example", to such crass and uncaring politicans as Jan McKenna of Arlington, Texas, who was first elected to the State of Texas legislature in 1982, and has written or co-written bills imposing more severe restrictions on a woman's right of choice over her body or the constitutionally guaranteed freedom to read, than has any other legislator in recent history.

Jan McKenna, like other totalitarian tyrants from Hitler to Reagan, is convinced she has received a mandate to reshape America—or at least a part of the nation. Convinced that her philosophy is the only correct philosophy for a true and loyal American to have and hold, Republican legislator McKenna has determined that abortions have to stop regardless of cost in human suffering by the mother or the fetus. Among the worse enemies of women, Jan McKenna has introduced legislation that would require any woman under the age of 18 to receive permission from her parents before seeking an abortion—even if the woman under the age of 18 is married and does not live with her parents. Even if this young woman, or any other woman, receives permission to seek out an abortion, before she is to be given the right of choice in the matter of the destiny of her body and its organs and their functions. In effect, Jan McKenna has pontificated that a woman has not the sufficient intelligence to make a wise decision for herself concerning herself. This decision, it continues, is valid only if determined by parents or a male spouse.

Jan McKenna has more than one crusade, however. And like the blood-thirsty and cruel Christian crusaders of the European Middle Ages who rushed Jews into synagogues and barns to burn the edifices down on top of their alleged enemies, and who entered into the Holy City of Jerusalem where they butchered tens of thousands of noncombatant citizens by hacking off Jew and Moslem heads and draining the dying trembling corspes' blood into the nave of the Church of the Holy Sepulcher, Jan McKenna slices at the realities she will not accept for herself. And, like a new god born from the dung heap of tyranny, she is determined to march ahead and strike down all opponents until enchained to her will and drugged mercilessly with her ideas which they in true clone fashion repeat like so many cookoo clocks all striking midnight repititiously until infinity comes to an end, Jan McKenna applauds the radical right and frenzied fringes of religious activists who demand an end to the separation of church and state. As reported in the Arlington, Texas *Daily News*, on Monday, 4 February 1985, in an article by Jon Weist, Jan McKenna gets her support from the religious activists who object to the lack of religious values—which must be read as *Christian* values—being taught in the classroom of *public* schools, regardless of the fact of the growing number of *nonChristian* students attending the schools. Since Jan McKenna and the religious radical right has not been successful in bridging the gap separating church and state in Texas, Jan McKenna, Republican legislator to the State of Texas Legislature, has introduced legislation into the Texas House that not only permits unlicensed teaching in private homes in Texas of Texas children, but also excludes any mention of any independent testing by public schools of the students who are taught at home by their parents and any other unqualified, untrained, and unlicensed "educator". This was essential to please the radical right, and Jan McKenna was successful in persuading Republican legislator Bill Blanton of Dallas to withdraw his bill which would have permitted in-home schooling, but which required occasional testing by public schools and recognized educators and education officials. Jan McKenna justifies her theocratic ideas and pronouncements by harping "We're reaffirming the fact that the freedom of religion guaranteed to us by the Constitution is more important than compulsory education."

It is Jan McKenna of Arlington, Texas' religious fundamentalist views which permeates everything she does politically or otherwise. This phobia of too much human freedom even slops over into her idea on what people can read or view. While she lauds and calls upon the Constitution of the United States to protect and guarantee her religious rights and freedoms, she refuses to allow others the same opportunity or correlatives. She is to be free to read her religious literature, but if anyone choses to read what she considers "pornographic" that is to be forbidden by law. Exactly what "pornography" is remains uncertain, except that Jan McKenna equates nudity with pornography, and human reproduction and the means to the propagation of the human race as tantamount to pornography. It is true that the main thrust of her arguments are aimed at sexually explicit materials which can be obtained in select and distant literary emporiums, but Jan McKenna attempts to lump all "disagreeable" literature and *objets d'art*—ranging from photographic stills to videos and motion pictures, and the like—into the same catch-all. She is, in the spirit of the Supreme Court's earlier ruling, attempting to "set the standards" for what "the community defines as obscene." The only problem with this is that she is attempting, covertly at the moment, to be the entirety of that community, legislating morality for everyone—including those who do not hold her rigid puritanical standards and ideologies. Jan McKenna will have her freedom but she is determined that no one who disagrees with her will be free.

Jan McKenna, the ayatolloah of Arlington, makes to pretense that her bill is vague. But as she told Reporter Weist, it is written so as to make it easier for "enforcement agencies to shut down X-rated movie theaters and video-tape distributors." She said spunkily, "I think it's going to make it much easier to prosecute" "smut peddlers" with her bill becoming law—a possibility she sees as having an excellent chance since it was referred to the House Criminal Jurisprudence Committee, chaired by Austin Republican Terral Smith.

Jan McKenna is set on mind control. She will set community standards. She will determine what other people read and see. Or, at least this is her goal. Hopefully Jan McKenna's legislative proposals, if they become law, will be struck down by the Supreme Court as being unconstitutional, and infringing upon the freedom of the American citizen—in Texas and everywhere.

Jim Norwood
To Be Censor—or To Be God

Jan McKenna is not the only ayatollah of Arlington. She is joined by an ideologist comrade in arms in the person of Jim Norwood who has been elected to the City Council and is determined to force his beliefs on personal lifestyles of anyone and everyone who lives in Arlington—children and adults, regardless of their views, desires, or beliefs.

Jim Norwood is against "sin." "Sin" is whatever **he** does not believe in. There is no need for public consensus—*he has the Truth.* He brooks no disagreement for he has a direct line to divine revelation and inspiration. He is the watchdog for god, and his god is a jealous god who will tolerate no opposition to Jim's near-papal pontifications. Jim and god walk hand-in-hand, fighting foot-to-foot in combat against corruption and evil.

Councilman Jim Norwood describes himself as a "born-again Christian." He has earned a reputation as a crusader against homosexuality which he believes quite narrowly to be a "sin" as well as a mental disease.

Homosexuality is a primary fruit of sin—the sin of not agreeing with Jim Norwood's interpretation of Christian canon which Jim Norwood defines as the Protestant Bible. As Councilman Ken Groves declared to the press, Councilman Jim Norwood is "attempting to legislate the morals of the residents of Arlington. He wants to take what he believes and force it onto other people."

Staid and ossified, Jim Norwood refuses to accept the plethora of reality. His reality is to be microcosmic to the point of being nearly micrococcus in nature, with his opinions enshrined in hardened tablets of law.

Disregarding the Constitution of the United States, 37-year-old auto paint shop owner Jim Norwood quickly became embroiled in issues concerning human sexuality, following his 1984 election on a pro-homeowner platform. Vehemently he has denounced homosexuality and homosexuals. In his abhorance of homosexuality he has attacked anything representing or supporting homosexuals or homosexual rights. He led in the verbal abuse of manager of the city's community theater when the manager prepared to produce a gay version of "Who's Afraid of Virginia Woolf?" (even though critics argue that homosexuality is the issue of the play). Norwood was also in the forefront of the fight to end "lewdness" in Randol Mill Park *among homosexuals*—eventhough he had next to nothing to say about heterosexual lewdness in the same park. Supposedly, in Norwood's thinking, homosexuals are incapable of genuine affection between consent-

Jim Norwood

ing gay adults, and, in line with the same reasoning, the sole reason for homosexuality is for promiscuity in a sexual sense—in total contradiction of all basic psychological treatises, research and investigatory writings.

Towards the middle of February, 1985, this demigogue determined to restrict the sale of material he personally considered "pornographic." While the original Greek word *pornography* (from *porne*, a prostitute, and *graphein*, to write) meant "the writings of prostitutes," Norwood defines it more narrowly to mean "sexually explicit materials" which have the "intent to arouse sexual desires" as if all "sexual desires" are not only immoral but unnatural.[1]

Norwood does offer the sop that those individuals who should desire to read or obtain pornography could do so through the mail, he does not want it (*i.e. Playboy, Penthouse, Hustler*) available at convenience stores—even though the convenience stores do keep such material behind the counter and will sell it only to adults who request it. To restrict the store owners evenmoreso, Jim Norwood proposes a change in zoning statutes in Arlington. Adult magazines, video tapes, and movies are to be sold only in industrial-

---

[1] For a different interpretation on the merits of *Playboy*, in opposition to the objections of Jim Norwood, see " 'Playboy' content is worth defending," by Rich Heiland, Arlington *Daily News* (3 March 1985) 4-A. Heiland takes the position that *Playboy* "is without peer in the United States today as [a] journal of fiction, commentary and general interest items. With the possible exception of *New Yorker* [magazine], there is nothing to touch it."

Heiland continued, "When Norwood seeks to ban *Playboy*—and that is what is being sought, rhetoric aside—he is not, as he says, banning pornography. To be sure, there are naked women in the magazine. To be sure, there are articles which discuss sexual activities and there is humor that a good many people would find offensive. But, there is much more there, and to relegate it to a sleazy store in a "combat zone" is to very directly banish

ly zoned locations that are at least 900 feet from a residential neighborhood, school, or church. This would effectively prohibit convenience stores which operate in residential areas to sell such material since, under the Norwood proposal, they would be denied permits to continue to market such material.

Councilman Groves pointed out that zoning laws are intended to regulate land use—not to worthy writing, whether by intent or misguided action."

Heiland praises the various authors who have been interviewed: "Bette Davis, Luciano Pavarotti, Blake Edwards and Julie Andrews, Dudley Moore, Sam Donaldson, Ted Turner, Earl Weaver, a group of Sandinistas, the *Hill Street Blues* cast, Kenny Rogers, Dan Rather, the *60 Minutes* crew, Wayne Gretzky, Moses Malone, Joan Collins, Calvin Klein, the Rev. Jesse Jackson, Shirley MacLaine, Jose Napoleon Duarte (the president of El Salvador), Paul and Linda McCartney, Goldie Hawn, Tom Selleck and Steven Job, creator of Apple Computers," as well as President Jimmy Carter. Established writers have authored significant articles and stories for *Playboy* as well; this stellar cast includes: "Stephen King, Arthur Clarke, Joseph Wambaugh, Ray Bradbury, John Updike, Anton Chekkov, Dan Jenkins, Robert Sam Anson, Arthur Schlesinger, Jr. David Halberstrom, Eric Jong. Paul Erdman, Ray Blount, Jr., Jules Feiffer, Hunter S. Thompson, William Manchester, Buck Henry, the late Truman Capote, Art Buchwald, Irwin Shaw, Reggie Jackson, Ron Reagan (yes, the President's son), William F. Buckley, Jr. (Yes, Mr. Conservative), D. Keith Mano (Yes, the former columnist for Buckley's *National Review*), Larry L. King, James Baldwin, Dick Schaap and Steve Martin."

The authors of articles in *Playboy* are as diverse as is humankind, a point graphically detailed by Heiland, who rejects the tired and scientifically unproved arguement of the alleged "moral majority" of demigogues such as Norwood who argue that the majority of magazines, like *Playboy* fall into the hands of impressionable young people. Furthermore, this lone voice of reasoned sanity who valiantly attempts to cry out for justice and freedom in the staid and ossified Arlington wilderness of bigotry and restriction, argues that he finds "video games installed in these [convenience] stores more damaging to my children in terms of wasted money and time," as well as "junk food and pop more damaging that *Playboy* or *Penthouse* behind the counter."

Norwood's arguments against showing "X-rated movies" at the University of Texas at Arlington does have a modicum of support. Alleen Stephenson worries that "they might affect the morals of young people," while Jeff Cartwright suggests that "as long as it's shown aftger nine, I have no problem [with the movies]." Kelli Ferris, taking a totalitarian chauvinistic approach totally rejecting the basic principle of democracy founded on the right to choose, pontificates as a new god, "That's disgusting [X-rated movies]. They can go to Fort Worth ... if they want to watch them. I don't think they should be at Arlington—especially at a state university."

eliminate a magazine from general circulation. As Groves ponders, "If you get started restricting one magazine, who makes up the list?" and, correlatively, once the list has begun, where does the list end? Furthermore, to regulate the sale of magazines under Norwood's proposal is unconstitutional inasmuch as it specifies an area which in effect bans the magazine's distribution on a limited basis without demonstration of just cause since it is not banned universally, as Fort Worth attorney Art Bender presented (*Dallas Times Herald* 19 February 1985, p. A-13). Norwood ignores such arguments. He will have his way and the public be damned!

True to the brilliance of a bountiful bovine, City Councilwoman Dottie Lynn supports the totalitarian and dictatorially undemocratic proposals of Norwood. Crassly she reports a support of "the intent" of Norwood's proposals—but in ox-like manner this sacred cow declared she would not cast a vote in favor of any regulation that might leave the city vulnerable to legal reprisals. Such is the stake of democracy in Arlington, Texas—where personal ideology is more important than the civil rights of all.

The real danger to the Constitutional civil rights of Arlington citizens, was graphically expressed by the crusty Councilwoman Dottie Lynn, as reported in 20 February 1985, *Arlington Daily News*. She confessed, candidly, "I guarantee you there's no greater prude on the council than I am," and swore that her prudery would become the gospel for those she represented, in the same manner as she dissuaded her children from watching nudity on television—by dropping oranges to distract the youngsters. Regally, as if she were living in ninth century Gaul, Dottie Lynn entoned her *Te Deum* and affirmed her willingness to support the limitation on the First Amendment of the United States Constitution in Arlington—once she was assured that her actions would be "on solid ground."

The limitation on the freedom to read and to choose was further glorified by Mayor Pro Tem Gary Bruner, who expressed a hearty support for Norwood's Grand Inquisition and Limitation on Pornography. Riding the waves of reactionism, Bruner brow-beat "the intelligensia or free thinkers or whatever you want to call them," for wanting to read "adult literature." His purpose, he declared draconically, was to protect the community standards that he somehow miraculously became the interpreter and spokesperson for. Councilman Ken Groves was the sole freedom fighter who gave zealous battle in defense of the Constitutional guarantees. He reminded his inattentive audience that the city attorneys had judged in December that the proposed Norwood ordinance was illegal and unconstitutional. He commented, sagely, "I, for one, am not willing to concede to any government, particularly a city government, the right to tell me what I can and cannot read." Lynn and Norwood ignored this spirit of Americanism, this outburst of patriotic fervor and righteousness by entrenching themselves in the stagnant and brackish backwater of reactionary mind control.

On Saturday, 27 April 1985, Jim Norwood, joined by Kenneth Vaughn, Susan Gray and a motley crew from Trinity Baptist Church of Arlington who seek an end to the separation of Church and state and by their actions call for the establishment of a fascist inquisition to weed out dissent and freedom to read, came out publicly in demonstration against the guarantees of the First Amendment of the United States Constitution. Demanding that the Southland Corporation's unit 7-11 stop selling literature which he and members of his radical right movement feel to be pornography. Calling for the wholesale removal of what he considers objectionable, he once more placed himself as arbitrator of morality, and defined his godhead judgement as that which would bring in elements of crime.

The sinister goon squad of Norwood, Vaughn, and Gray, harping on their insistence to police the thoughts of free citizens, determined to block the development of understanding and enshrine the concept that ignorance is bliss, raced on to urge a boycott of the stores (such as the 7-11 located at 5704 Green Oaks Boulevard in Arlington) which did not cater to their petty vested interests. These totalitarian dictates by these select hoodlums, hopefully a minority in Trinity Baptist Church, have germinated into a call for the City Council to overpower private businesses and dictate exactly which sorts of products they can sell and where they can sell them. If Norwood and his calloused crew pull off this enslavement and bondage of human liberty, by specifically banning *Playboy* and *Penthouse*. his list will undoubtedly expand until any literary work which does not meet his autocratic demands is prohibited not only from being sold but from being read even by mature and rational adults in the privacy of their own homes. Norwood supports his open attempt to play censor and god in Arlington with the undocumented, unscientific and unproven charge that the magazines he objects to are falling into the hands of children. He quotes spurious and scurrilious scrutum societies, such as an alleged national "decency" group that unsubstantiately declares that no less than 70% of "all adult magazines" fall into the hands of the young. Yet, this demigogue of Texas does not offer any reference as to where they get their "facts" from, for in truth they have no source to support their tyrannical diatribe devoid of all reality or social justice.

The bottom line of the aspirations of Kenneth Vaughn, Susan Gray, and Jim Norwood is that they want to control the lifestyles of those around them. They want to determine what people read. By controlling what people read they will control what people think, how they act, and what they believe in. In order to do so, to dictate their values upon others, they mean to close down private businesses which do not support their fascist demands, even if it means an end to free enterprise: an end to the basic principle on which America was founded, fought wars over, and men died for.

Openly Norwood and his gang are working to push select Arlington ministers into the dubious roll of being ayatollahs—who promise a pogrom greater and more heinous than ever that feared in

Iran. Already these ministers are marshalling their forces to push through highly subjective concepts by means of handpicked candidates they endorse and sponsor for elective office. Democracy is to be slaughtered in Arlington on the stained altar of tyrannical theocracy, with the demon and demigogues of self-righteous orders ruling pontifically from a dais set up over the broken pieces of democracy.

Contrary to Norwood's protestation that censorship is necessary to protect the young, and his vitrolic pontifications that it is up the conservative element in America—to whit, the Republican Party—to stem the tide of rising "pornography," several prominent Republican Washington Congressional Representatives, such as Pennsylvania Senator Arlen Specter, have publicly questioned the censorship of such magazines as *Penthouse* and *Playboy*, reminding Americans that there is no evidence that the material covered in these magazines, be it photographic or literary, that leads to child abuse or child molestation. Instead, these leaders caution Americans from attempting to curb the First Amendment or face the inevitable possibility that the First Amendment will be done away with all together and no one be permitted to read or view anything that does not fall into the censorial hands of a few limiting demigogues who will go on to attack the remainder of the Constitution and its Amendments until America languishes under a despotic dictator worse that seen in other totalitarian states around the world, similar to the undemocratic tyrannical forces popularly known as the Contras of Nicaragua who fight against all liberties, freedoms, and rights of self-determination in their bloody effort to control the minds and lives of people to serve their vested selfish interests leading to personal enrichment while impoverishing the masses, forcing the people of Nicaragua into a state of illiteracy and indifference while supporting the return of a Somoza dictatorship.

Urban Pettiness
& the Denial of Democracy

No city, anywhere, is without bigotry, or immune from calloused consciousness, but a few cities—or more precisely—towns, have an exceptional amount of pettiness and bitterness towards the handicapped and less fortunate. At the top of the towns which discriminate is Cleburne, Texas, which has gone to the Supreme Court petitioning for the right to discriminate against the mentally retarded. Discounting the reality that those mentally handicapped are citizens with equal rights under the law as any who are not mentally handicapped, and who are capable of functioning in a meaningful manner within society and being productive towards and with society, albeit possibly on a more limited basis, the crassness of calloused Cleburne carries the coffin of hate filled with the cadaver of human rights staked through the heart by a draconic debilitation of democracy directly aimed not only against the mentally retarded of Cleburne, but against the very fundamentals of the American Constitution and the individual right to express individual choice in the pursuit of happiness.

Since the close of the 1970s the city of Cleburne has battled with two women: Jan Hannah and Bobbie Northrop, to keep the mentally retarded out of an earth-colored stucco house five blocks from the granite Johnson County Courthouse, where in their case, democracy is decried and dragged into the dungeon of hate and irrational fear. The primary principles set forth by the framers of the American Constitution are now bastardized. The very freedoms which were fought valiantly by the soldiers of liberty in the past two hundred years are mocked by the City Council of Cleburne, who tyrannically tied a noose around the neck of justice by issuing zoning restrictions against the proposed home for the mentally retarded, whom in the collective ignorance of the City Council of Cleburne label as "mentally deranged" in a feigned attempt to hide their own simple-minded prejudices.

A ghost-town in the world of living liberties, Cleburne, Texas machiavellianly argue that their unjust laws must be preserved as holy, harking back to the ante bellum thesis that the most rudimentary law on the most limited and narrow scale is of greater value, importance and praised worth than is any national legislation or universal philosophically accepted credo. The injustice of the hardened hearts of the City Council of Cleburne, Texas, comes to rest on the dung-heap of "states rights" versus human rights, where it is no longer the South versus the North, but the house on Featherstone Street versus Cleburne.

Neither Jan Hannah nor Bobbie Northrup had any idea that when they attempted to create a group home on Featherstone Street, they would be imbroiled in a nationally celebrated case of contemporary bigotry, against a city where any rational person would think twice before relocating and bringing up children. In an effort to afford equal opportunity to all, Northrup and Hannah kicked up a maelstorm over the rights of the retarded—a volcanic explosion which pulsed past local interests to land in front of the highest legal bench in the nation.

Financially unable to champion the cause of democracy themselves, the two women of Featherstone Street received the assistance of a handicapped rights group located in Austin: Advocacy, Inc., who sought legal remedy and support. But due to the growing self-interest of the legal system in Texas where Yuppie mentality demands the escalation of the rights of a few vested interests over the rights of many, U.S. District Court Judge Robert Porter of Dallas ruled in Cleburne's favor in 1982.

With the take over of the White House by the radical Right, the cause of freedom for the mentally retarded seemed lost. Politicians who sought reelection began to parrot the ante bellum arguments which divided the nation one hundred years earlier. But not all justices espoused the narrow hegemonic self interests of the radical Right, and the women were heard by the 5th Circuit Courts of Appeal in 1984, who in April of that year overturned the lower court's decision.

The City Council of Cleburne was not to be outdone. The City Fathers called out for a new trial to assert and demand a vindication of their jealous localism, boyaristic bigotry, and denudation of democracy, so that their petty principality of personal vindictiveness would continue to lay under the myriad of the debris of their mentality.

The City of Cleburne was not without its supporters. The Reagan Administration came like a dark knight charging in on the back of a dinosaur of reactionism to champion the cause of the City Fathers. Under the direction of the former Hollywood actor, Ronald Reagan, the Reagan Administration filed a brief in the case, arguing that the mentally handicapped—unlikle blacks and other minorities—are not a class that deserves special attention to prevent it from suffering discrimination. The Reagan Administration, in fact, argued that the mentally handicapped deserve pity—not protection, in an satanic attempt to revert back to the days of an America before the advent of Dorothea Dix.

Continuing Reagan's policy of stepping back into the nineteenth century, such antediluvian demigogues as Dick Armey of Denton, Phil Gramm of College Station, John Leedom of Dallas, and other radical reactionary members of the lunatic fringe of the Yuppies have enslaved the Republican Party, long stifled under George Strake. The Reagan Administration, linked with the government of Cleburne, openly argued for a reversal of the national trend to bring the mentally retarded out of institutions and into the community, in settings such as group homes, where they could be no longer an economic burden on society but, in any small way, be a asset bringing limited skills into the market place. It was, as testified by the national Association for Retarded People and eleven other advocacy groups which supported the Featherstone experiment, "an ordinanance ... for state-imposed segregation." And it was more. For the City of Cleburne was denying the national trend towards greater personal freedom. While the number of group homes across America had spiritedly jumped from less than 700 to more than 6000, Cleburne preyed on the movement as if to be the high priest of social injustice and keep Texas at the bottom of the advance, for in Texas there are only 107 group homes—and Cleburne wants no more—even though a federal court not yet controlled by the draconic Reagan Administration demanded previously that Texas move more than 9500 retarded citizens currently in institutions into group homes.

Cleburne, Texas, is not without co-conspirators, for the cities of Galveston and Lancaster have also piled faggots of hate and bigotry around the altar of justice, waiting to kindle the fires of intollerance into a mighty conflagration until liberty is burned beyond all mortal recognition. Their individual laws are archaic and blatantly discriminatory, harkening and heralding justly the feeble-mindedness of the communities in which they are enacted.[1]

The problem of Cleburne is that a few select businessmen who fear the loss of a single dollar more than the loss of the freedoms guaranteed by the American Constitution feed the fear that rumbles without logic through the hearts and minds of the citizens. Louis Zimmerman, who led the charge against the principles of the Constitution of the United States, declares that the proposed home was a threat to the community since it was "right across from the school [Cleburne Junior High School]," and implied that mental handicappedness might be contagious and affect those who would want to learn.

Louis Zimmerman continues to drag out nineteenth century arguments in his attack upon the mentally handicapped. He is convinced that the mentally handicapped are "like children" who need to be constantly watched. He entoned, "if they [one of the potential residents] got out in the street, they'd get run over. There's no place for those people there [across from the school]. They should be at the edge of the town, where they can have room to run around."[2]

Zimmerman's anger is carried into the courts by Dallas attorney Earl Luna, who represents the town. He argued that the city had the moral and spiritual obligation to discriminate against the mentally handicapped, since "the city has a responsibility to prohibit unsanitary and inhumane conditions," and argued that because of the size of the proposed Featherstone home, and its location across from the Junior High School, "the group home was unsanitary and inhumane, and the city had a rational basis to deny it."

Yet, by state law, the home meets all requirements. By federal law, the proposed home for the mentally handicapped meets all standards for space and amenities. The injustice brought against the mentally handicapped by the calloused City Council of Cleburne, articulated by their attorney and other spokespeople, is a notorious attempt to discriminate based on irrational fear— at the same time human beings who are American citizens wait patiently for a home of their own and the fulfillment of the American dream where they can attempt to be their best self, contribute to the commonweal, and be a strong statement of the continuing dream.

As the Dallas *Times Herald* detailed, Kelly Watson "wants a home like anybody else." Cleburne denies her even this simple right and freedom.

The City of Irving follows clitelumic Cleburne in its antipathy towards the mentally retarded. The move to close La Mancha, a fourteen bed home for mentally retarded youth, became possible when the Texas Department of Health cancelled its funding for the home at 408 West Sixth Street, after Medicaid revenue dried up (the payments accounted for 66% of the home's funding).

The decision to refuse funding for the home is one more nail into the coffin of civil rights in

---

[1]Texas law requires special permits for "hospitals for the insane or feeble-minded." The Featherstone project is not a hospital, and thus does not fall under this restriction, leaving the fact therefore, that the Cleburne position is openly discriminatory.

[2]Dallas *Times Herald*, 18 March 1985, A-7.

Cleburne's attempt to tyrannically misrule, passing a dictatorial ordinance against human freedom for the mentally retarded was rebuffed and rejected on Monday, 1 July 1985, by the United States Supreme Court. In a 6-3 decision, the US Supreme Court ruled that the city of Cleburne was acting on "irrational prejudice" when it denied a permit for a home for mentally retarded people, reversing a 5th U.S. Circuit Court of Appeal's Yuppie ruling that would have made the mentally retarded a "quasi-suspect" class of citizens.

Texas. It is also another shovel of dirt against the national image of Texas in the area of social services, which has rightfully earned the ingnominious distinction of being ranked 48th in the nation in per capita expenditures for aid to the mentally ill.

The closing of La Mancha is only a part of the lost beads of benevolences from the necklace charity—now a naked gnarled noose of broken promises the State of Texas made to the mentally ill. Another link was severed when a home for 6 to 12 year old emotionally disturbed children was closed in Dallas' suburban area known as Oak Cliff, a homey, tan brick building located at 1353 North Westmoreland.

Known as Hillside, the fifteen bed treatment unit for disturbed children run by the Dallas County Mental Health and Mental Retardation Center on North Westmoreland was scheduled to close on 31 May 1985 due to a funding crunch. This finalized when the Dallas County Commissioners declined to vote $877,387 for its upkeep when Medicaid payments were stopped by Reagan. It's fourteen occupants are to be displaced—but no one knows where they will be resettled, if they are resettled at all. (The children who live at Hillside are a special case. They are troubled children who have come from abusive homes, and in retaliation against the personal abuse they have experienced at the hands of friend or relative have become dangerous to themselves or to others—threatening suicide, sexually assaulting other children, or setting fires. More than other mentally disturbed children, these children need constant and immediate supervision, care, and love—all which is to be denied them with the closing of Hillside)

In both situations, as it has been in other cases of homes being forced to close because of financial difficulties, the blame justly falls upon Ronald Reagan who repeatedly denies federal funding for the mentally ill. Although Reagan is convinced that the individual citizen will "dig deep into his pocket" to keep the homes going, and to afford the mentally ill a promise of hope and future cure and care, the stark nakedness of reality hits hard—charity is the ugly and unwanted stepchild of the average citizen. The rejection of charity is to become even more prominent, since Ronald Reagan announced his intention to do away with the income tax deduction for charitable contributions, giving validity to the judgement of Eileen Bruni, a local advocate of the retarded, who declared that "this is the obvious result of Reagonomics."

This criminally calloused conduct of the Reagan Administration[3] has not "saved the citizens' money." Despite his theatrics, Ronald Reagan's windfall savings he believes he has captured by cutting programs to the mentally handicapped, will reap for him the whirlwind of a greater need for society to take care of the children they forget today when the morrow comes. Ronald Reagan and the conservative Radical Right, strangling the Republican Party in America have forgotten that the children denied

---

[3] See my *Reagan & Woman* (Dallas: Texas Independent Press, 1984).

care and opportunities to grow and become at peace with themselves will be the chronically ill adults of tomorrow that Texas society will have to support or incarcerate.[4]

Discrimination in Texas is not limited to either Cleburne or against the mentally retarded. Discrimination denying democratic due process even to abused children also exists in Texas, draining the milk of human kindness into a cesspool of self-protection and non-involvement.

Residents of the town of Arnett, which lies a few miles west of Gatesville on U.S. Highway 84 (it is so small that it doesn't even appear on the official State Map of Texas), does not want to admit the existence of child abuse, nor does it want abused children housed within its geographic limits. Like seventeenth century Salem, the residents of Arnett fear the unknown, and will do everything in their power to stop it.

As if witches were flying on broomsticks, and goblins were haunting vacant houses, the residents of Arnett are prepared to wage war on the "forces of darkness" which seem to threaten their very existence. They will give bloody battle against "the intruder" who is unnamed—but which is a group of Gainesville residents who want to convert the vacant Arnett Baptist Church building into a placement center for abused children.

---

[4]See my *Tomorrow's Tyrants: the Radical Right and the Politics of Hate* (Dallas: Monument Press, 1985).

The battle ground is a stereotypic field of the elderly against the young. The majority of Arnett's citizens are retired, and feel that the "do-gooders" of Gainesville are attempting to "push" them around, as G.T. Whitley explained in his defense of the local organization which is trying to keep the center out of Arnett.

Few Arnett residents believe that the proposed shelter for thirteen young people would be a "halfway house". Instead they see it as a potential den for juvenile delinquents—even though the center would have nine staff members, including two counselors who would work full time at the center, with the "houseparents" watching the children around the clock, being careful not to let any of the children roam throughout the local neighborhoods.

Arnett residents suggested, that if the home was granted a permit, it be required to build a "high fence." This saphrophagous sentence was made on the sarcophic assumption that the youth would want to flee the home, and thus give foundation to their fears that those who would come to the shelter were in fact delinquents. The problem with this reasoning is that once the center was approved, the agency would prepare information packets on prospective center residents, and the board members would choose which children would be best-suited for the center. The proposed center would not be a "dumping ground for juvenile delinquents, as Arnett citizens enshrined in a verbal garbage heap.

Dallas *Times-Herald*, 25 February 1985, D-3.

Harkening to antediluvian puritanical standards where any expression of human emotion or display of human anatomy was denounced as being a testimony of satanic intent and evil, the Euless City Council on Tuesday, 26 February 1985, cavalierly enacted two reactionary ordinances limiting the adult's individual freedom of choice, freedom to read, and accompanying first Amendment rights as a statement of total contempt for human dignity and civil liberties. The Euless City Council acted as if directed by Jim Norwood of Arlington.

Extreme rightist Chairman of the City of Euless Advisory Board for Social Concerns Henry Boatright, promulgated in the manner of the sixteenth century Czar Ivan IV Vasillievich, Grand Duke of Muscovy, a rigid standard to determine and outlaw obscenity that "might fall into the hands of" Euless' youth. The ordinances were in response to those convenience stores which refused to obey his ukase to stop selling adult magazines or wrap them and keep them behind the stores' counters.

In the manner of a spoiled, self-centered child and anointed neo-Yuppie, Boatright demonically demanded that the Euless City Council adopt a confining convoluted code of "morality" contravening specific Constitutional rights of the citizen—modeled after the obnoxious, odious ordiance orchestrated against human dignity and self-determination by the Dallas City Council which robed itself in psuedo-self-righteousness, prohibiting the sale and display of "obscene material" within 1,000 feet of schools, churches and residential areas. Like dumb cows following a raging, bellowing bull, the Euless City Council unanimously bowed obsequiously before the throne of Boatright and adopted his two toxicosis terminations of the First Amendment, silently lauding the preparatory draft by Euless City Attorney Bob McFarland. Although the Euless Or-

Bob McFarland

dinance did not use the exact wording of the McFarland-Boatright emunctory document, it did effectively meet his provisions and wishes, eventhough its ultimate result may easily be encephalomyelopathic for Euless in general. Pity the future generations!

The provisions of the ordinances prohibit the sale and display of graphically described human sexuality. It does not address pornography depicting bondage, abuse and violence, sex and sexual/gender stereotyping, racism, bigotry, or other forms of the diminuation and debilitation of human dignity and fundamental human worth.

While sexually explicit magazines are now banned under the Grand Inquisition of Euless, popular magazines such as *Penthouse* and *Playboy*, for the moment, remain available for the public to buy and read without fear of punitive action inflicted by the City Council. At the same time no mention is made of such magazines as *True Confessions*, *War Record*, or *Bondage* which openly laud, graphically illustrate, and subtly, covertly encourage the reader to sadomasochism, rape, violence and blood-shed. All that the City Council of Euless was concerned about was magazines which carried photographs or drawings (but not the written commentary) on any part of the human anatomy in a state of excitement. The new ordinances specifically prohibit the depiction of sexual activity, as well as the depiction of the sex organs in a state of arousal. The new ordinances also prohibit the display of any items which depict such things (*i.e.* posters, display racks, advertisements, and the like).

Taking a totalitarian stand against freedom of choice and the right of the adult individual to read and view any material, City Attorney Bob McFarland has taken on the crusader's cross to champion his brand of censorship, and passed on copies of his ordinance to the city councils of Bedford and nearby communities. His next goal, as was recorded in the 27 February 1985, Arlington *Daily News* (3-B), is to sit in judgement of what movies will be shown at the University of Texas at Arlington (they are supported by student fees). It is as if he were running for the post of Grand Inquisitor, his lips coldly set against any expression of human worth or drive that he personally considers to be obscene.

The real problem with Bob McFarland, as it is with Jan McKenna and Jim Norwood, is that neither he nor they understand the intent and purpose of the First Amendment. In his, and their drive to end "pornography," they, in essence, are attempting to ban that which is merely disagreeable to them. But what is or may be disagreeable to this unholy trinity of self-annointed demideities is or may not be disagreeable to another or others.

The argument of McFarland, and well-meaning other demigogues who want to ban that which they find objectionable, as being beyond the understanding or knowledge of the Founding Fathers, don't know their own history. Pornography, using McFarland's definition, was especially rampant in the seventeenth and eighteenth centuries—ranging from the bared bosoms and sexually implications subtly glossed over in "The Rake's Progress," by William Hogarth

(1697-1764), and the nudes of William Blake (1757-1827; an English mystic and poet), to the risque writings of Jean Marie Arouet Voltaire (1694-1778). Even Benjamin Franklin penned several pieces of eroticism which would never have passed the McFarland test—yet were read and applauded by nearly all of the Founding Fathers who signed the Declaration of Emancipation and consented to the publication of the Constitution.

McFarland, like the vicars of Arlington McKenna and Norwood is not, it is apparent, interested or concerned with history or human freedom, but intent on legislating morality and taste regardless of whom he hurts or what freedoms he abridges or destroys. If this is accomplished, what is to happen to the basic principle of freedom on which America was founded—that we are to be free to read, worship and speak as we choose, and be free from the imposition and intrusions of the state in our private lives.

There has been a fall-out over the Norwood, McFarland and McKenna explosions. Their bombardment of words promising a holocaustic vengence on those who do not think as they, has intimidated University of Texas at Arlington President Wendell Nedderman to slaughter academic freedom upon the pyre of bigotry and censorship, plunging the dagger of insensitivity to the arts into the bosom of freedom of expression while castrating the blossoming of opinion, leaving it a carping capon crawling listlessly and in void on the desert of the university campus. As if he were a character from a Feodor Mikhailovich Dostoevski novel, this Grand Inquisitor has odious trappings of a muscarine high priest to stop the mind from thinking, the eye from viewing, the tongue from discussing that which does not please him if information and awareness of the forbidden fruits are enjoyed upon "his" campus.

Sitting as High Priest and Judge over the University of Texas at Arlington's film board, Nedderman has banned all "X-rated" movies from being seen "unless the movie is part of a legitimate academic or educational program." With parched lips he stated further that all X-rated movies student leaders would want to show in the enrichment series will require the consent of the administration. Among the voices of sanity raised on this issue is that of Student Congress President Mamie Bush who argues that most UTA students support the idea of free choice and oppose the new censorship aimed at limiting if not stopping the guarantees of the First Amendment of the United States Constitution. A referendum on the capricious and insensitive unAmerican policy of Nedderman was called to be held on 17-18 April.

Nedderman's support comes from a small group of the religious radical right on the UTA campus, headed by Greg Sullivan, president of the UTA Baptist Student Union. Leading a small demonstration outside the student theater during the showing of *Emanuelle: the Joys of a Woman*, offered 25 January 1985, Sullivan set himself up as god to blast the film as immoral, and with his gang of zealots distributed a petition to ban X-rated films. His petition was signed by only a few hundred students, less than even a tenth of the student body, but the signatures he collected were sufficient for Jan McKenna of Arlington to rise regally in her seat at Austin to call upon Nedderman to institute the ban. Tearing down the principles of freedom of choice and right to read, Jan McKenna was quickly joined by Arlington Republican Senator Bob McFarland, and warned against any affirmative action responsive to the letter of the Constitution.

Goaded by the pressures of Norwood, McKenna and McFarland, Wendell Nedderman stepped away from the august principles of academic responsibility, and as if silently cursing justice and freedom of choice, indicated that he would ignore any adverse referendum.

It is interesting to note that Nedderman's ukase comes at a time when Arlington's political clime is volatile. At the same time it is both a capricious and an illogical policy since the University of Texas at Arlington shows between 70 and 80 films a year, and "X-rated" films are given only at a ratio of 1 out of every 50. Rarely has more than a single "X-rated" film been shown in any year.[4] Thus the censorship of Nedderman is, at best, a move to appease the radical right of the Texas legislature which controls academic institutional funding. Money has spoken louder than human rights which McKenna, McFarland and others would sacrifice to build their own ideological empire.

---

[4]John Moritz, "UTA movie ban draws fire," *The Arlington Citizen-Journal* (7 April 1985) 9A.

Under the machiavellian cloaking disguise of religion, James Curtis, a University of Texas at Austin student, heading a gang of four from the UTA Baptist Student Union, marched against the American Constitutional guarantee of freedom to read, coldly labeling their totalitarian tactics as "Christians Against Porno." Even though Curtis was not required or subjected to view any cinema offerings of the Student Activities Board Film Council series, Curtis charged against the natural right of other students to make a choice freely and democratically. Attempting to justify his proposed tyranny at the University of Texas at Arlington campus by claiming that he was marching with a plethora of students, the truth was that all four of the democracy-denouncing demonstrators were Baptist Student Union members, and were openly attempting to impose their morality on others.

Bowing before the political pressures put upon him by Jan McKenna and Bob McFarland of Arlington, University of Texas at Arlington's President Wendell Nedderman gave into the dismantling of freedom of expression and the prostitution of academic independence. The position taken by Nedderman overwhelmed the community, turning the issue into a political football, with the small radical group of students at the Baptist Student Union playing forward and tackle.

Running over individual freedom, using the mind destroying cleats of the threats of Bob McFarland, who (according to the Arlington *Daily News* Friday, 5 April 1985, p. 5-A), threatened legislative action to ban the films if the university did not take action, Nedderman called the State Senator to help draft his guidelines for what the students at the university could see without university or state censorship. Nedderman's reactionary action put the advance of educational freedom back to the dark ages in the history of education, tacitly affirming the principles preachificated by McFarland and McKenna that the university is not independent of its surrounding and the public and that freedom to think and to learn is limited by what the state dictates capriciously and without reference to or respect for individual judgment.

Wendell Nedderman and James Curtis are wrong. The issue isn't over pornography but freedom of choice, as the referendum at the University of Texas at Arlington on Wednesday and Thursday, 17-18 April 1985, showed that 74% of the student population at UTA did not "oppose

Wendell Nedderman

the showing of X-rated movies on campus," and 66% believed that "X-rated movie ban is an infringement upon" personal rights. Even more critical to the issue of human freedom and mature adult responsibility in line with the exercise of choice was the third question, "Should students have the right to decide to view X-rated movies on campus?" Champions of democracy, 87% of the students affirmed this basic right, while only 13% fell in line with the radical minority who wanted strict censorship and mind control at the University of Texas at Arlington. As Bill Forisha, chairperson of Students Rights in Government sagely observed, the results of the referendum show conclusively that the issue is not X-rated films but freedom of choice which Wendell Nedderman is desperately attempting to control and destroy in a most heinous and totalitarian manner smacking of the very essence of pure fascism. As Forisha said in an interview with local media, "The results of the third referendum really brings out the point we're trying to make. Our objective is not to get X-rated movies on campus, but to make it a matter of free choice. This is a First Amendment-type issue" a guarantee of the American Constitution which Nedderman and Curtis are waging war against. Vowing to stand firm as freedom fighters in the manner of the Founders of American Liberty, the students at the University of Texas at Arlington are poised to give battle against the mephistophelean moans of radicals in the Baptist Student Union aligned with Jan McKenna and Bob McFarland who have pressured Nedderman to relinquish his duties as defender of academic and human freedom, coming out against the very people he had sworn to support and uphold.

Students fighting for freedom to learn and the right of choice in the media they view began circulating petitions the last week of April to overturn Wendell Nedderman's totalitarian tactic of caligulaean censorship. The petition states that the university students, of which the average is 24, should be allowed to determine and decide their own personal moral values and not have the moral values of select demigogues of Texas be forced upon them against their free will.

Correctly the concerned scholars at UTA have realized that the issue is an infringement of their rights, and concluded that the cause of Nedderman's undemocratic ukase was a direct result of the inappropriate and hostile pressure by Sen. Bob McFarland of Arlington, who the petition acknowledges to be an "insensitive public official." There was little doubt in the minds of many UTA students that McFarland misused his position on the Senate Finance Committee to "buy" support for his censorial banning of films that he determined to be "pornographic" although the legislator disclaimed such a thesis and argued that he did not "pressure" Nedderman by threatening to withhold funds from the university.

McFarland's tactics however leave question as to the strength UTA has to withstand an onslaught of radical right pressure. The thread of democracy at UTA, already weakened by Nedderman, is close to breaking. The student's actions in the last week of April are aimed at restrengthening the fibers of freedom that Nedderman and McFarland choose to sever.

For centuries institutions of higher learning have fought valiantly against state interference and the right of its students to learn. Wendell Nedderman, with a stroke of the pen, ended that valiant effort and gave birth to a potential promise of increased state censorship, limitation on reading and thinking, and a possible return to an era which saw Galileo Galilee silenced for expounding an unpopular and societally rejected theory (that the earth revolves around the sun), or the sixteenth century Spanish-born theologian and physician Michael Servetus, who questioned the power of the state and was executed by John Calvin and his band of religious radicals.

Wendell Nedderman has devolved himself to the nadir of being like Innocent III—personally weak and unwilling to defend the principles for which his office was created and he was entrusted. Academe in Texas suffered its first great blow with the crumbling of Nedderman's resolve.

The City of Garland

Racism is alive and well in Texas. It thrives in large cities and small communities. It is especially flourishing in the Dallas suburb of Garland.

The Austin Middle School is acknowledged to have superb teachers. The average size class is only 10 students. The administration is caring, and a basic peace permeates. Yet the families who live near the school are divided, with the caucasians refusing to have their children learn beside Mexicans and blacks — less than 10% of the school is white, for Garland, entrenching and deifying racist bigotry has adopted a statute that permits "freedom of choice" which officially allows students, but in truth permits parents, to choose where they will attend school—provided it is within the same district.

The petty-minded bigotry of these families in Garland goes unchallenged—eventhough the United States Supreme Court ruled that such a situation was unconstitutional. Justice in Texas is buyable, and as late as February 1985, there has been no effort on the part of state or national

Justice Department lawyers to take action to force whites to attend the black school (the sole dissenter in this situation is the people's champion, Attorney General Jim Mattox, whose home is in Mesquite, next to Garland, who began an investigation into this affront to human dignity, in 1984). The age old ignorance of pigmentation remains fertile and people in Garland and elsewhere throughout Texas continue to believe that a person's skin color determines their mental and moral standing and ability.

Even Garland blacks have taken no action. Although they formed a local chapter of the NAACP (National Association for the Advancement of Colored People), they have yet to file a legal challenge to the unforgiveable plight at Austin Middle School. As individual citizens the Garland black community has done nothing, as well; for no black parent has come forward to demand an end to the rampant racism in the district, nor to demand a change in the school policy. Thus segregation grows stronger daily, and the possibility of a violent end to the advances for racial integration into a commonality that spurred many on in the days of social concern of the 1960s becomes increasingly inevitable—to the loss and detriment of the the maturity of Texas.

Even the economics of racism fails to inspire any Garland resident. Quick to protect their money as seen in the turnout of the number of voters who voted for their pocketbooks in 1984, the residents of Garland choose to ignore the magnitude of the destruction of their pocketbooks when it comes to racial segregation. Austin

Middle School is costing the Garland residents more than any other school in the nature of tax dollars, as only 142 students attend the school in 1985, eventhough when the building was erected, it was raised with the purpose of seating 720 students.

Deanna Beale, a white mother, makes no pretense of her racial bigotry. Her children will not go to Austin Middle School because "There are a lot of blacks at Austin."

Ken Barnes, who lives across the street from Austin Middle School will not let his children attend it. He argues that the school is run down and the students are constantly in fights. Nothing is further from the truth, but when ignorance attempts to justify bigotry and hate, any excuse seems plausible. The actual situation is much more different, for the district has spent $130,000 on renovations since 1980: including new cafeteria and gymnasium floors, new cafeteria tables, a new clock and bell system, retiled walls and new paint throughout.

The one serious problem with the Austin Middle School is that its students do not have an equal opportunity to learn. Much of this is because Austin Middle Schools suffers from deprivation in its library resources, funding for teacher improvement, and an inadequate staff. Furthermore, Austin Middle School is the only school in the district without a modernized science laboratory, expanded library space, and improved art and band rooms. But with the enrollment figures dwindling, there is little interest to upgrade or improve existing conditions. Bigotry is expensive.

Dr. "No" —
The Problem of Dick Armey

Refusing to spend one cent of America's massive wealth to feed a starving child, and voting against every single piece of important legislation introduced into the 1985 Congress, Dick Armey, Republican Representative of Denton, found time in the evening of 25 March 1985, to cast his first affirmative vote to blow up the universe. Although individual health, freedom, and human rights means nothing to Dick Armey of Denton, the prosecution of a Hollywood style Star Wars is an overwhelming concern. Rather than see a smile on the face of a small child, or a look of gratitude on an aged person who has finally been given sustenance, Dick Armey applauds the wanton destruction of city and village, the annihilation of the human race (or any part thereof), and rejects as "unnecessary sympathy by bleeding hearts and liberals" any "give away program to the shiftless who must learn to take care of themselves" or starve slowly, painfully, agonizingly to death. Complementing Charles Dickens' *A Christmas Carol*, Dick Armey lauds the theme that if a person cannot work then let that person go to a work house or starve, for the world would be better off with less of its surplus population.

Armey's vote against aid to Ethiopia was decidedly anti-family, as noted by Democrat Representative Mickey Leland of Houston—similar to the anti-family, ahumanistic attitude and voting pattern of Republican State Representative John Leedom of Dallas, who was one of three Texas State legislators to cast negative votes on the bill introduced to feed Texas' hungry (although the bill called for the expenditure of $14.8 million, that breaks down to approximately only $6 per day per person of those starving in Texas). Leedom repeated the tired claim that "Texans should open their hearts—it's not something that should be done by the state." To whit: if the people of Texas don't want to help the poor and destitute—let the poor starve.

A staunch and stagnant reactionary who boasts of his love affair with the economics of Adam Smith and the milieu of the eighteenth century when human dignity was pounded by *laissez faire* capitalism and its message *enriche vous* ("get rich [and the world be damned]") cast 22 negative votes in the House of Representatives during his short introductory three month tenure. He was the lone dissenter in a 413-1 vote approving bonuses for government whistle-blowers, (introduced by Democrat Congressperson Pat Schroeder of Colorado) arguing that the bonus would cost the government money—eventhough the whistle blown brought in previously "lost" revenue which vastly outstripped the extent and amount of the bonus. The bill itself was labeled, and acknowledged, as a cost cutter, and towards the end of the vote, when Armey's solitary "no" was about to make history in its own way, representatives of both parties approached the Denton radical conservative, asking him to change his mind. He refused, claiming that the bill was "bribing" civil servants "to do their job." Armey's attitude towards the starving of Africa was that such an appropriation bill was no more than "a short-sighted, almost knee-jerk reaction to the plight..." while admitting, "there are starving babies in Afghanistan, there are starving babies in Nicaragua, there are starving babies in Kampuchea [Cambodia]" but warned that America can not feed them all as "we have a scarce amount of aid that we can give," and so it would be better to let them die.

The 44-year old former university professor (North Texas State), who holds a doctorate in economics, and built his campaign to win a congressional seat with the apology that he regretted having wasted his time as a teacher, has not only attacked aid for the poor, food for the starving, and financial assistance for the dwindling and impoverished American farmer—programs which he considers to be "budget-busters" that Congress cannot afford when the Reagan deficit is now the highest in history, soaring dramatically past $200 billion and increasingly daily with the each unnecessary and wasteful MX missle which is built, but he proposed to rename the Civil Rights Act of

1985 the "Comprehensive Government Intrusion Act of 1985," and venomously vowed to vote against it. "Blacks and wet-backs [Mexican-Americans] already have too many rights," he told a small crowd of loyal supporters in Denton, who cheered his resolve and pledged to stand by him in his "fight for the American way" as originally detailed in the scenerio of the Ku Klux Klan.

The Civil Rights Act of 1985, which Republican Representative Richard Armey labeled "the worst bill that will come up in this Congress," would insure equal voting opportunities, work to overcome discrimination in the market place, to afford housing opportunities and the freedom not to live in fear—assets which Armey labels liabilites. Armey opposes this proposed legislation since it is designed to overturn a 1984 Supreme Court ruling that narrowed coverage of a law banning sex discrimination in federally assisted education programs (*Grove City College vs. Bell*).[1] Laws barring discrimination based on age, race, and handicap were also affected by the Supreme Court decision. Armey defends his discriminatory ideology with the argument "That bill is so open-ended that very literally no area of our lives is safe from the government being involved. That bill is really awful."[2]

Armey is not content to let the poor starve, or to build the weapons of destruction which can erase the human race from the planet earth, but he is convinced that small businesses are not

---

[1] See my *Reagan & Woman* (Dallas: Texas Independent Press, 1984), chap. 2, *passim*.

[2] Dave Montgomery, "Armey's not a 'no' man for nothing," *Fort Worth Star-Telegram*, Sunday 24 March 1985, A2.

necessary to the American economy. At the forefront of the radical conservative forces in the United States Congress, Dick Armey proposes to abolish the Small Business Administration. With his eye towards what he defines as solid economics for the nation, this Denton legislator argues that the abolition of the Small Business Administration would be a blessing for America, and that America would save $5.5 billion dollars by abolishing it—which, he reasons, would be "enough to buy the MX [missile system] three times." Getting rid of the Small Business Administration, furthermore Armey contends, would be to "mercifully end the agony" of those small businesses and entrepreneurs who were not able to make a significant profit (regardless if they were making a profit of any size at all—including one which would at least afford them a minimal livelihood)." Armey places his opposition to the Small Business Administration and towards small businesses in the same dungeon of chaos and irrationality into which he descended when he sacrificed the small farmer, claiming, "Fifteen percent of the farmers [in America] are so deeply in trouble now that all we are doing with this [proposed] bill which he voted against and Ronald Reagan eventually vetoed—before he joked that instead of exporting grain, America should export surplus farmers] was prolonging the agony. There is not a farmer in the world who doesn't know its more humane to shoot a dying horse than to let him live."

"When you have a hopelessly painful situation," Armey continued, it's better to put an end to the situation rather than prolong the pain."

Richard K. Armey

Insensitive to the growing poverty in Texas, "Dr. No"—Republican Representative freshman Congressman Dick Armey has sponsored legislation that would award tax breaks to businesses while penalizing labor by reducing the minimum wage from the current $3.35 an hour to $2.50 an hour for teenagers who seek summer employment. A strong Reagan supporter, Dr. No has detailed a series of "budget cuts" which would disenfranchise many adult laborers, deprive farmers of needed revenue for spring plantings, and deny women the right of personal free choice, by seeking to end the Small Business Administration, Job Corps, Amtrak, and forever squelch the ERA and prohibiting legal and safe abortions, silently suggesting that it is better for women who carry an unwanted fetus to self-abort with the use of unsterile clothes hangers, or seek out the butchery of an untrained practioneer whose office is the dark stench and garbage filled alleys of Texas' slums.

While Armey objects to increasing federal taxation he is in favor of new tax breaks that could reduce federal revenue and thus make large-scale deficit reduction more difficult. Among the measures that he supports—which would directly increase the national deficit—is legislation that would allow parents of substantial means to set up tax-free individual retirement accounts of $1,500 a year to pay college education costs of their children—a luxury only the wealthy could indulge in since the middle class and poor worker has a difficult time just making subsistent expenses of housing, food, and transportation. Coupled to this proposal is his movement to double income tax exemptions which would further reduce the American treasury and make debt repayment not only more difficult but slower in occuring, so much so that the accumulating interest on the debt would become backbreaking and possibly unpayable. At the same time Armey proposes a freeze on Social Security payments, and has suggested reducing the payments which would help those least capable of sustaining life without government assistance.

Against those who support clean air and the utilization of natural forms of energy over proliferation of nuclear generating plants, Dick

Armey is supporting a move to abolish the Synthetic Fuels Corporation, which provides federal subsidies to companies developing new energy sources. This wiley representative of ultra-conservative yuppie views and self-centered interests at the same time is supporting the end of the SFC he wants to revise the licensing process for nuclear power plants, significantly reducing the time it takes to get them operating license and thereby increasing the possibility of a nuclear action and the potential for nuclear holocaust. Obviously human safety is less important to Dr. No than is the economic advance of businesses which support his political aspirations.

Dick Armey has little knowledge of or concern for the safety and preservation of Planet Earth. Following the Reagan line, Armey argues for strength through exhaustion, wasting our precious natural resources on a nuclear Maginot Line and, with blustering advocacy, inviting sabotage and terrorism while leaving us open to the same. He supports the irrational and irresponsible Star Wars program of the Reagan Administration—a costly device that will stretch this new and destructive Maginot Line across the universe, past the Milky Way and into new galaxies—where, if life exists, all can easily be destroyed by the hands of Earthman.

Congressman Richard K. Armey promises America security and prosperity. Yet freshman Republican Armey endangers the global economy by raids upon its limited resources that must last as long as humankind has a future by his constant willingness to misuse its resources for nuclear power and the promise of a possible Armaggedon. Armey refuses to conserve our natural resources, to defuse the population bomb that can go off any moment as the world's poor continue to produce unwanted progeny that has little to eat and practically no hope. Armey continues to defile the only place in our known universe which has life on it by coming out against ecological protection programs, cutting back on budgets for natural resource protection, and arrogantly ignoring the environmental issues of clean water, clean air and open space.

Joining with Reagan in assaulting the earth magnifies inequities, escalates tensions, accelerates anxieties and adds to the supertension that can produce chaos at home and abroad, lead to violence in the street and the rape of the countryside, if not even to that fateful nuclear result of an unacceptable and undefendable Armageddon known as Nuclear Winter. Is it truly the will of the people of North Texas to have acid rain fall upon their homes, fields, pets, and individual lives? Is the individual's pocketbook's prosperity more important than peace, dignity, and human rights? Dick Armey has numerous supporters who say no—money is so much more important than all the civil liberties that are currently being enjoyed that the Congressman enjoys attacking and dismantling with a sword rusty from bye-gone centuries when Adam Smith ruled the economic world with his distorted and dangerous philosophy that spoke for the rich and against the poor. Armey delights in referring to himself as one of Smith's most ardent supporters, and Smith's world is to become the future of Texas.

Supporting Dick Armey's attempt to marshall forces to strip Americans of traditional freedoms are several Texas Congressional Democrats whose only interest is in their political progress and prowess to dismantle constitutional civil rights. Democrat Sam Hall of Marshall, among the most self-righteous and self-serving Congressional Representatives who unswervingly supports the most henious plots of the Reagan Administration to transmorgify America into a class stratified and starved society, has repeatedly urged a limitation to a woman's freedom of choice, rejects homosexuals as human beings, refuses to consider necessary funding for major medical research in epidemic areas, and jousts with the basic principle of separation of church and state. He is joined by Ralph Hall of Rockwall who sneers at such concepts as equal pay for equal work, denounces the rise of women's awareness movements, and blasts the right of citizens to determine their own destiny. Sam Stenholm, the most self-anointing Democrat in the House of Representatives is quick to support big business, justify the erasure of self-determination of Latin American people if they choose a political system he opposes—even if their choice is expressed in a free and unopposed election—and demands near adulation of his pet projects. Marvin Leath of Marlin makes Mussolini appear like an angel, with his constant insistance to legislate against those who interfere and oppose his standards since they do not concur with his messed message of hate and bigotry. His hollow backbone supports a cancerous cadaver of economics that enrich the rich and devastate the poor, for his god has become wealth and his priest those who pray to money.

The federal government has become too big for these Texas demons and demigogues who argue that Washington has interfered with the process of bargaining between labor and industry. They applaud the Reagan Administration's goal to reduce minimum wages, and the anti-labor pro-subsistent income measure feignedly known as "Right to Work" (for less!) which feeds the entrepreneur from the table of the employee, stripping the worker of dignity, right of choice and redress, and the opportunity to develop personal skills and professional conduct leading towards direct involvement in business, industry, or farming. But self determination for the masses is not on the agenda of these Democrats who find the true meaning of "democracy" unbearable and in a twisted and transmorgified sense "un-American."

Like the small, grayish, long-snouted beetle *Anthonomus grandis* of Mexico, known in Texas as the "boll weevil," whose destructive larvae hatch in and damage cotton bolls, these vicious vipers and self-serving satanic serpents suck the life blood from the poor for the benefit of the rich, demand sacrifices from the least capable to be layered around the bulbously fat necks of the wealthy, while feathering their own dung heaps of petty personal prequisite politics with the few comforters created by the struggling masses yearning to be free of their tirades and charades pretending to support the principles of democracy and freedom. Not since the late 1890s, when the American Congress was at the mercy of tyrannical titans subject to the mercy of robber barons who controlled the trusts and interest of America has this nation or this state of Texas suffered so much from so few for the sake of those least deserving.

No less than one out of every five children in America lives before poverty. Hunger is a daily occurance to these Americans. Congressional Budget Office chief Rudolph Penner admits that they will experience the damage of poverty for years to come—a poverty Reagan and his Administration are indifferent to

The current poverty level is greater than it was in the mid-1960's when President Johnson attempted to cure America's hunger with his commendable Great Society programs. Now it is getting worse.

Black children are almost three times as likely to be in the poverty group as white children. And, more than half of the 13.8 million children living in poverty in America are in families headed by women whose rights are daily curtailed by the Reagan Administration supported by such radical right members of Congress as Dick Armey of Denton.

Insensitive to the needs of the people of Texas, U.S. Republican Senator Phil Gramm and the Texas GOP frantically telephoned conservative state lawmakers Wednesday, 29 May 1985, urging them to vote against a measure to provide health care to the poor. Money, as always, was more important to these demigogues than health *of the poor.*

Coldhearted partisan politics were conducted as usual among the conservatives in the Austin legislature. Monied interests outstripped the needs of the poor, generating the GOP to produce a large block of opposition on key votes.

While the GOP aligned with conservative Democrats were digging another grave to bury Texas' poor in with their self-righteous gold shoves of personal privilege, Texas legislators Helen and Ray Farabee of Wichita Falls struggled against seemingly insurmountable odds to gain support for the needy who are unable to afford adequate medical attention. Laurels of victory were soon there when the tie vote was broken when the Speaker cast the deciding vote.

Ronald Reagan
& Texas

Ronald Reagan won the electoral college vote of Texas in the November 1984 balloting. He won by a simple majority. This by no means indicates or firms a mandate. Yet Reagan argues that he received a green light to pursue his reckless military spending while cutting back on internal betterment programs from the people—policies which in reality are aimed against the general populace and will help only the limited few. Those most dramatically hurt by Reagan and his Administration are the farmers—especially the small farmers.

Prices for crops have been historically low. The decline in agricultural prices has plunged the farmer deeper into the never-ending pit of American economic collapse. The farmer is saddled with an escalating national deficit which is made more unbearable by the expenditure of unnecessary and fiscally irresponsible and unsound MX missiles—a boondoogle that enriches a few while threatening the lives and economics of many—during the Reagan Administration. This was but one reason that Reagan did not do as well in the rural voting areas as he did in the urban areas plagued by a surplus of self-serving young urban professionals.

On Monday, 4 March 1985, a growing number of America's farmers had enough of Ronald Reagan and his misadministration. Leaguing together in a common cause, those who put bread on America's tables, met in Washington to protest the disinterest in American farmers by the current Administration. At a demonstration sponsored by the American Agricultural Movement, civic conscious citizens blasted the President and his attitude of indifference to the plight and lot of America's food growers. With considered preparation and measured speech, the sage Senator from Iowa, Tom Harkin, concluded that Reagan "has a screw loose," affirming the analytic judgement of Congressional Representative Dan Glickman of Kansas, who detailed Reagan as "a direct threat to agriculture in this country."

The harshest criticism of Reagan and his Administration came from the diminutive Texas Agriculture Commissioner Jim Hightower, who dismissed Reagan's farm policy as "economic genocide." In the populist genre, Hightower suggested that "Ronnie Reagan is living proof that you never get too old to find another way to be stupid;" he continued his thesis offered to the one thousand plus farmers who gathered on the steps of the Jefferson Memorial by saying, "but we are the ones who are having to pay a price for his stupidity." To support his contention, Texas Agriculture Commissioner Jim Hightower detailed the President's general lack of knowledge of the problem, his total ineptness to appreciate the structure of farm costs in relationship to realized revenue, and then concluded that Ronald Reagan is "a Hollywood fabrication over there who is blithley pursuing a policy of economic genocide against the very people who are putting dinner on his table right now."

"Now, I know that a good number of the farmers and ranchers voted for Ronnie Reagan in 1984," Hightower acknowledged. "That's because Ronnie Reagan was promising us a seven-course dinner. Now, we figured out what ours is: It's a possum and a six pack."

Although Hightower primarily leveled his salvo of words against Reagan, others in the Texas delegation did not fail to note that a significant percentage of the blame for the Reagan abortion of the farm came from freshman Senator Phil Gramm of Texas, a professor from Texas A&M University at College Station who had argued in his campaign for John Tower's Senate seat: "it's the rich who suffer" while he blasted the poor with the argument "it's only in America where the poor are fat"—ignoring medical evidence that majority of the "fat poor" are that way because of their diet which is almost exclusively restricted to calorie-heavy starches.

Marion Garland, Texas State President of the American Agriculture Movement criticized the junior Senator, saying, "Phil Gramm is completely out in left field. He's just parroting the administration's policies."

Other Texas demonstrators condemned Gramm for voting against a farm credit bill that had been approved by the Republican led Senate. They were particularly distressed with their Republican Senator Gramm for tacking on to the bill an amendment that would have prohibited any necessary spending on the farm bailout measure if it "increased the federal deficit." Yet, eventhough Gramm was worried about the farm bill increasing the federal deficit, and basing his rejection of the farm bill on the potential that it would increase the federal deficit "even marginally," Gramm had no hesitation voting for the economically wasteful expenditure of monies on the MX missiles Reagan lusted after to compliment his Star Wars program.

Reagan's overt lusting after a nuclear war has ended the lives of numerous farmers—not from natural causes, but from self-inflicted suicidal wounds. Self-inflicted gun-shot belched out death in 1984 and ended the life and farm labor of 53 year old Cecil Morrison, Jr., of Deaf Smith County. A similar situation took the life of 51 year old Freddy Lesly of Crosby County, Texas, in 1982. Their suicides culminated a long battle to avoid financial ruin brought on by the Reagan Administration, which has brought over the past four years with a promise to continue the next four years, increase in depressed and declining prices for agricultural commodities.

But suicides are not the only result of the Reagan Administration's handling of the farm crisis of the 1980s. Alcoholism is on the rise—as is depression, divorce, and physical violence against family members and the friends and neighbors in the rural communities. Carl King, executive director of the Texas Corn Grower's Association, relates the daily parade of farmers which trek through his Dimmitt office, many in tears as they watch their savings and work vanish after stockpiling a small fortune for 30 years. The physical and mental stress that he witnesses, he details as future heart attacks and high blood pressure bouts—many of which are fatal. Firmly he believes, "there's more suicides in agriculture now than ever."—a diagnosis confirmed by Sue Smith of the Alcoholism and Drug Program for the West Central Texas Council of Governments.[1]

The majority of the problem centers on the medium-sized commercial farms, or family farms. Large corporate farms, or farms run by "week-end farmers"—those who have other jobs in industry and/or business—do not suffer as much. But suffering still occurs, and it is in dramatic where more than 1 out of every 20 farmers in America lives. Texas farm experts predict that nearly one-quarter of the medium-sized commercial farms will be financially forced out of business by the end of the current year.

The growing agricultural decline and accompanying poverty is affecting many an older Texas farmer fatally. Instead of seeking counseling, the older farmer man and woman turn inward, close themselves off from their friends, ministers, and in some case, their families. Giving way to depression they become listless, sometimes schizophrenic and even catatonic. Depression and loneliness, a psychological suicide, ultimately ends their misery.

The tragedy of this is that Texas State Republican Chairman George Strake argues that "the farmers made their bed," and that "it is not the duty nor the responsibility of the national government to bail them out." Calling for increased farm support for the radical farm-destructive measures and plans proposed by Reagan, Strake urges Texas farmers to "forget the little annoyances" and "back the GOP, crossing over into the party which speaks for Texas," always failing to admit that the GOP speaks for limited, vested interests of those who feel that the American farmer is a burden on society which must no longer "be supported, bailed out, or helped."

The arsenic arrogance of George Strake comes when he complains of his food bill, blasts the Texas farmers as being "short-sighted," and yet demands their continued allegiance and support—in spite of the fact that the Republican Party platform, drafted in Dallas in Summer of 1984, decreed "Family farms are the heart, soul, and backbone of American agriculture; it is the family farm that makes our system work better than any other." This absurdity has a promise of being around for a long time—for this is the policy of Ronald Reagan and his administration, summed up in the casually caustic and calloused comment by Budget Director David Stockman cemented in the history of the winter of 1985: "What's a small farm? That's a sociological concept." The farm is, to Stockman, a joke, and an academic point—it is not the reality of men and women, young and old toiling for a living, working under hot sun and in cold rain and wind, to feed themselves and America, and to continue the tradition of countless forebearers before them. The farm is to be sacrificed on the scrap heap of broken promises issued at the Republican Convention by those demigogues who would rule America for the amusement of the wealth and corrupt. Reagan's war-lusting UN ambassador Jeane Kirkpatrick babbles on about the "San Francisco" Democrats" in her labored message of hate, saying nothing about the plight of the farmers and the other truly needy in America which the GOP has chosen to relegate to the status of a stepchild to be placed in the cold ashes of its fires of destruction.

Tartly troubled trebuceted trematodiasis words tumbling from the lavendar lazarus lips of some Reagan supporters decried fellow farmers who complained of the treatment they were receiving from the incumbent national executive office, declaring that "We're going to have to bite the bullet" and "get back to a market-oriented program"—a program which has not worked in America since before the depression of the 1920s-1930s. But a "free market" in the 1980s is a myth. In part this is the result of government interference in agrieconomics, but for the most part it is the result of a fluctuating world economy, escalating interest debts burdening the farmers farms (which have declined from 2,949,000 in 1970

---

[1]David Pasztor, "Finances shred fabric of farm life," Dallas *Times Herald* (25 March 1985) A-10.

to 2,370,000 in 1983), a dwindling farm population (while the national farm census fell from 9,712,000 in 1970 to 7,029,000 in 1983, in Texas the farm population collapsed from 806,000 in 1970 to 269,000 in 1980), land inflation, foreign competition, and the net national debt which has risen to catastrophic proportions under Ronald Reagan who has been frequently called President Deficit.

Farm exports have peaked. Compared to the $43.8 billion realized in 1981, 1983 holds a promise of only $36.5 billion. This disintegration of foreign markets has been the result of an increasingly strong dollar—making American farm commodities less attractive to nations which have less capital to spend on the products. Because of this the majority of America's farmers, and the farmers of Texas market their goods to the national government since under current price supports they can realize greater gains by selling their surplus crops directly to the government, instead of lowering their prices to meet the foreign market's ability to pay. To lower their prices in order to compete would be disasterous, and their losses would be even more staggering, throwing more than 45% into bankruptcy—instead of the pronosticated 25%.

Like Phil Gramm and Dick Armey, David Stockman of the Office of Budget Management, and Ronald Reagan argue that many farmers will fall under the back-breaking and mind destroying stones of bankruptcy which will take from them and their children their farms, homes, tools, livelihood and self-respect. Stockman calls this situation a "natural realignment" in the world of free enterprise and business economics, synthesising his discompassion for the American farmers with the conclusive pronouncement: "but that's the way a dynamic economy works."

Bad weather, low crop prices and high interest rates have especially strapped the farmers southwest of Lubbock on the plains of Texas. Numerous families are averaging a $10,000 loss per year, and have done so for the last four years, making their ability to qualify for refinancing of existing loans difficult, and securing new credit for the spring 1985 cotton planting almost impossible.

Texas farmers in the Panhandle are facing not only economic loss, but even the physical loss of their topsoil because of minimal rainfall. Many farms in the Panhandle have only dry water wells to show for years of determined care and drive to make a living for themselves and their families. More than 140 mid-size family farms are now facing both bankruptcy and foreclosure. Some have giving up all hope and are voluntarily liquidating their dreams, landholdings and other assets. Blatherskitic bankers are reluctant to issue or extend existing credit since they cannot guarantee investors a return higher than those paid on U.S. Treasury bills—a return many investors are demanding.

The Farm Credit System, operating as a pipeline from the money market to the country, and regulated by the federal government eventhough it is privately funded, has been increasingly reluctant to fulfill its stated purpose of farm investment with the decline of farm land valuations.

Because of this, it is predicted, that farm debt will rise by 7.5% in 1985, while income will realize only a 6.5% increase. This increase cannot off-set the $210 billion national farm debt.

The most logical solution to this problem, overlooked by the Reagan Administration, and rejected by such demigogues as Dick Armey and Phil Gramm, is to institute a national policy, to be backed by similar measures on the state level, of limiting crop overproduction. This can be done by penalizing surplus production through a system of taxes—or by means of withdrawing existing tax exemptions. Such a program is similar to that first introduced by Franklin D. Roosevelt to stem the tide of foreclosures brought on by the Depression. It is more logical than fining farmers who overproduce, because their basic plight is such that they have no money with which to pay a fine, but, on the other hand, taxing future revenue generated by overproduction will act as a psychological deterrent since excess production will, correlatively, bring increased taxation. At the same time, the government (both on the state and the national level) should raise crop prices to a minimum level where they equal no less than the cost to produce them. This would be a national "floor" for the crops sold to the consumer, who if in the business of distributing crop productions for refinement or use could sell at the same price or greater. Although, initially, such an action would be inflationary, it would increase the Gross National Product (GNP). And, once such a program was established, production of surplus crops limited, and pricing stablized, farmers would have a greater and more regular income with which to pay their debts and the interest on their loans. Once that farmers were given an opportunity to get out of debt, the psychological malaise affecting the farm community would decrease, family ties strengthened, and a new *elan* would be born again.

To ask a farmer to voluntarily limit his crop production is nonsense, for the individual farmer would be afraid to do so on a solitary basis since there would be no assurance that neighboring farmers and farmers throughout Texas or the United States would voluntarily limit their own production as well. Therefore it has to be done by the governments of the states and the national government, for the Constitution specifically empowers Congress to make laws for the good and the protection of all American citizens.

Although there is certainly a chance for some illegal activity, such as one farmer overproducing in an effort to gain greater revenue, policing action can still be achieved by reviewing records of commodity procurers and the like.

Taxing overproduction is more effective than paying for nonproduction, as payment for nonproduction is tantamount to paying out something (money) in return for nothing (nonproduction). Such action is an insult to the men and women who cherish working, and find dignity in farming. Since few people enjoy paying taxes, taxing overproduction produces an incentive not to produce more than the market can bear.

Foreclosures, however, are not limited only to farmers in Texas and throughout the United States. Merciless banking interests regularly have foreclosed on personal homes since the days of the Depression of the 1930s, with an increase in the number of foreclosures escalating under the Republican ascendancy of the 1980s. Ronald Reagan's first term saw a spectacular rise in the number of foreclosures. While 1993 homes were repossessed in 1982 in Tarrant County, Texas, the number of Tarrant County homes which were taken from their owners jumped to 2891 in 1984. In Houston foreclosures have been averaging 2000 a month—although 1985 predictions have the number of foreclosures rising to no less than 3000 a month. San Antonio residents have been, so far, more lucky, with only 200 families being shut out of their homes by lending institutions each month (the Dallas rate is approximately 425 a month).

Along with home foreclosures comes sheriff liquidation sales of household furniture and possessions—unless the debtor seeks protection in the federal court system by filing for bankruptcy. Bankruptcies are at an all time high—with the federal docket not only full, but overflowing. Nothing is being done by the Texas legislature to assist the people of the State of Texas who are facing not only financial ruin, but also the total loss of everything they have, precipitating suicides, family fights, murders, and physical abuse of wives, husbands, children, relatives, neighbors, and animals.

Farmers and householders will be joined in their desperation by the youth of Texas if Ronald Reagan is able to get through Congress his crass proposal to lower minimum wages for teenagers. While the President calls this proposed disabling legislation "a youth opportunity wage," in reality it is a subminimum wage which will encourage many employers to fire the parents of the youths who are making at least the legal minimum in favor of hiring the teenagers at the touted wage of only $2.50 per hour for work done from May 1 until September 30 over the next three years.

To make this polarizing plan acceptable to many minority leaders, Reagan enlisted the aid of articulate spokespeople who travel the state in an effort to win their support by claiming that the three year limit is only a "test" of the proposed legislation. Those who would benefit from such a pelargonic program would be the retail industry which would realize a windfall profit while decreasing its overhead, thereby escalating the extent of that profit. The one industry which supports the President's attempt to gain retailers cheap labor is the McDonald's Corporation—a fast food outlet which has historically been in favor of subsistence wages. McDonald's pays above the minimum wage only in those areas where the market demands it, for few teenagers are willing to accept minimum wage, especially if they are married, as the minimum wage will not, in most cases, even pay the month's rent on an apartment that has the minimum of comforts. At $3.35 an hour, or $134 a week before taxes buys little, forcing many teenagers into prositution, drug trafficking, and other criminal activities.

Until the youth of today can make a liveable wage, something the Reagan Administration does not believe is necessary, there will be increasing difficulties and divisions between the age groups, catapulting the anger of the young against the older generations when they are in a better earning capacity—creating the loathesome yuppie who would do away with all the basic protections today's elderly depend upon.

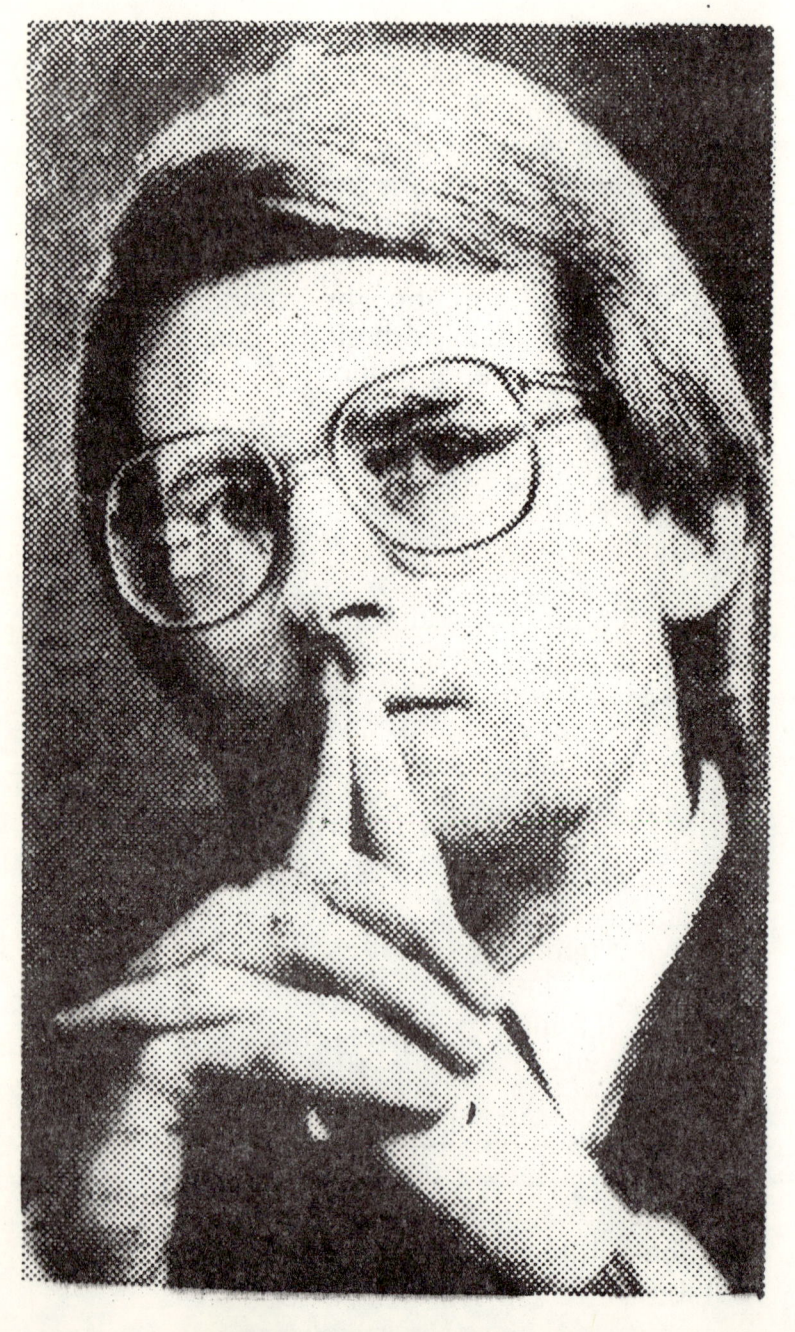

David Stockman

David Stockman and America's Farmers

The American farmer is unimportant to David Stockman—and to his boss, Ronald Reagan. National Budget Director David Stockman believes that the American farmer must be forced out of business in order for "a dynamic economy" to work. Addressing a Congressional hearing Wednesday, 14 February 1985, Stockman declared that many farmers will be forced out of work and off their farms, but affirmed his belief that this was a good thing for the national economy—and for the farmers themselves. Speaking for Reagan and the Office of Budget and Management, Stockman declared that farm subsidies and national farm programs put the nation into debt. To end such programs, Stockman sleazed, would bring America back to national solvency in the economic sphere ruled by big money.

While criticizing American farmers for not being economically productive, and at the same time lauding Ronald Reagan as the man of the hour to save the nation from creeping paralysis, David Stockman also confirmed that no less than one-fourth of the nation's savings and loan institutions had failed and gone out of business since his boss had been first elected in 1980. Immediately after this confession, Stockman acknowledged that up to 50% of all American auto production workers had been thrown out of work, but said that such action was necessary to force the auto industry to "adjust."

When Stockman was asked about the plight of the small farmer, and whether or not the Reagan Administration wanted to see the small farmer and small independent farms survive, implying that the small farmer must give way to the large amalgamated farm industry of corporate concerns run by machines and operated and owned by a select minority of established Republican rich. The days of the small independent farmer are numbered. As each Republican is washed into office in the tide of brackish backlashed water, the night of economic collapse begins to set.

While the *Washington Post* reported Stockman's address to Congress on the position of the Reagan Administration towards farming, the *Los Angeles Times* carried a piece on the plight of Iowa farmers, and how Iowa state officials and bankers were attempting to personally and collectively rescue 5000 farm families in the first months of 1985, while forestalling the demise of 50,000 more. The state legislature of Iowa proposed the establishment of an independent state agency to sell $60 million in bonds, the proceeds to be used to reduce or "buy down" interest on agricultural loans for one year—secured by a $150 million special account established by the state's 400 banks.

The Iowa Legislative action is only a temporary measure. By the first of 1985, experts estimated that no less than 40% of the nation's farm families were in immediate danger of falling into bankrupcty, giving proof to the Reagan lie issued by the Republican Party that "America is better off today than it was four years [during the Presidency of Jimmy Carter, 1976-1980] ago."

Ronald Reagan & Texas' Radical Right Politicians

America was founded on the principle of the separation of church and state. Our forefathers enshrined in the Constitution the right of all citizens to be free of church interference in their public lives, yet this guarantee is being rapidly eroded in fact by Ronald Reagan and the political action group known by the misnomer of the Moral Majority, Inc.—a corporation.

Ronald Reagan openly acknowledges that he bases his economic, political, social, and international policies on limited theological ideologies—turning to the collection of writings believed to be divinely inspired by a minority of Americans who profess Christianity. Less than 50% of citizens of America accept this literary work as inspired, yet the President proposes it as the guide to his government of, by and for the super rich—for the poor will discover their reward in heaven (so says his bible).

To silence potential opposition to his planned theocracy among assembled clergy and religious representatives, Reagan cited his book of divine inspiration before an assemblage of 4000 religious broadcasters who met in Washington, D.C., 4 February 1985. The "Evil Empire" (the Soviet Union), was cast in true Hollywood fashion as the brothel of Lucifer, and to keep Satan in his dominion of damnation, Ronald Reagan proposed an escalated preparation for a real-life Star Wars that would have made the mogul of California celluloid, Cecil B. DeMills, proud. Reagan justified his plan, pointing to Luke 14:31, which he exegeted showed that he was supposed to have more combat troops ready for war than was expected to be prepared by the Kremlin for the final Armageddon. His knowledge of Greek, like his basic undertanding of Soviet policy, is weak at best, and an understatement of understanding of human psychology.

Reagan's knowledge of theology is equal to his appreciation of world holy days. This was demonstrated during his speech in which he declared Scriptures support his defense buildup, when he recalled looking north from the White House during the Christmas season and seeing "the huge menorah celebrating the Passover season in Lafayette Park." Near the time of the Christian Christmas, the Jews actually celebrate Hanukkah—Passover is celebrated closer to the Christian Easter.

With stylized faux-grandiloquence Reagan's rhetoric is an opiate for a weary people who desperately desire succor, rest, and security—even at the risk of the loss of personal freedom and liberties. They are willing to give up their declining standard of living in hopes of achieving "peace through strength," arguing "arm to disarm", and agree to allow the already financially overweight Pentagon to swallow up more of America's resources while its citizens wallow in hunger and deprivation.

Reagan's proposed 1986 budget will eat into the very heart and drink deep of the pulsating blood of those who gave him his victory over the former Vice President from Minnesota. It will cut most deeply into the life line of the middle class, with farm supports being hacked away as banks greedily foreclose on farms, confiscating agricultural machinery and supplies while those who toil the soil are forced into an urban environment they do not know nor care for, to stand in growing lines of unemployed looking for honest work. At the same time the 1986 Reagan budget seeks to severely sever veterans' health care programs, while slicing mercilessly at the heart of student aid so that only the rich could afford an advanced education. Even Medicare is not to be spared, and federal employees are to have their retirement pensions limited, cut, and in some cases abridged, by penalizing those who retired before age 65 by subjecting the retiree to a 5% annuity reduction for each year they were under age 65. At the same time, Reagan proposed, to cut federal wages 5%, in spite of the fact the inflation is no less that and growing.

The one legislator who supports his plans without question is Senator Phil Gramm of Texas, who likened the cuts to a bitter pill that needs to be swallowed so that the patient [America] can get well." But one legislator, former North Texas State University economics professor Dick Armey, does not believe that Reagan has gone far enough. How much better it would be, as if Armey mused, if the world was returned to the days of medieval knights who rode roughshod over the small gardens of the poor in quest of the game of the forest only they could eat! or if business were unchecked, as they were at the turn of the century, being able to put out potted meats filled with sawdust, chopped mice and rats, and human waste. If business wanted a spokesman they found it in Dick Armey who rode into Washington in the garbage bags of Reagan, vowing to protect business, affirming that business was not to be taxed.

Dick Armey shows less compassion and human consideration than does Ronald Reagan. Acidly arguing for the enactment of *The Wealth of Nations*, this one-time professor, who in his campaign rhetoric lamented that he had ever been in a class room, came out against the poor with greater crassness than did even James Watts, Adolf Hitler, or Phil Gramm.

While Armey, Gramm, and Reagan mourn the terrible burden of taxation carried by business—at an all time low—the silver cloud of Reagan's prosperity has an increasing dark lining: more are in need than ever before. Whereas poverty had been cut dramatically in half in America during the golden era of the Kennedy and Johnson administrations, and remained at about 11% during the period 1973 to 1978, since Ronald Reagan slithered into public office 35.3 more million human beings fell below the poverty line. Simply put, that figure is the largest percentage in 16 years.

While Ronald Reagan and his coterie parroted the litany that "America is better off today than it was four years ago [during the Carter administration]," in the 1984 election of style (Reagan) versus substance (Mondale), the truth is exactly opposite. Unemployment in 1983 reached levels equal to those of the Great Depression of the 1930s, while in 1984 the majority of the jobs lost carried middle income salaries, while those which took their place carried subsistant salaries which could not keep a family at minimum standard of living.

Since 1978, 8 million American families have dropped out of the middle class into the chaos of poverty. Many have no home. Few have work. Divorce, prostitution, and drugs are rampant, and have increased dramatically with the advent of the Reagan Administration which continues the lie that things are getting better in America. In the last four years, during the "prosperity of the Reagan Administration," as lauded by Margaret Heckler, Secretary of Health and Human Services under Ronald Reagan, the real income of the bottom fifth of American families declined by nearly 8%. At the same time the income of the top fifth of American families rose sharply almost 9%. Dick Armey argues that this will spirit business to new heights to create jobs, afford better wages to its employees, and increase America's standard of living—in keeping with Smith's politico-social base philosophy—which stellularly didn't work in the eighteenth century nor can it today.

Minorities continue to suffer the most, even their numbers are increasing during this Dark Age of Reagan's Administration. The abandoned aged women, the divorced, the mentally and physically ill, the homosexual, the untrainable, handicapped, and racial minorities whose pigmentation makes them prime targets for employment exploitation, make the descent into poverty more dramatic as it delves more deeply, far more rapidly than ever before in American history. To this ever increasing number now comes the "blue collar elite" who had enjoyed salaries ranging from $25,000 to $40,000 a year, displaced from their jobs by the rise of automation, decline in demand for their products, and the increase in foreign competition.

Women suffer the most under Reagan. The number of single women raising families who live below the poverty line has escalated from 35% in 1982 to more than 40% in 1984. The young two-parent households have had a similar history, rising from 34% to 40% in four years, and continuing to march towards the opening chasm of unredeemed poverty.

Other statistics are as startling. 35.6% of all black American citizens live below poverty, of which 14.6% are elderly blacks. 80% of all farmworkers in America live in poverty under Ronald Reagan. The census role of the poor farmers are growing, their farms decreasing in number or are being stripped from them by bogtrotting bankers whose only goal is to enrich themselves until they too fall victim to the malaise of the Reagan Administration which is set on an irreversible collision course with universal destitution and impoverishment, while its leaders and the Pentagon wax more fat than the proverbial sacrifical bull.

While statistics do not always tell the entire story, 93% of the poor live on less than $5,000 a year. The greatest number of those who suffer this insult to human dignity are children and women, who can be counted the poorest of the poor. These unfortunates do not even have minimal diet, shelter, or medical care. As a top official of the United States Department of Health and Human Services, run by Margaret Heckler, former Republican Congressional Representative from Massachusetts, testified before a House committee on poverty, 408,000 families had lost all welfare payments 1982-1983 due to revised regulations promulgated by the Reagan Administration. An additional 557,000 human beings fell below poverty because of recent Reagan cuts in social programs, and the tide is swelling.

The Reagan Administration continues to issue the blatant lie that things are getting better. But, regardless of the crassness of the lie, statistics show that despite recent tax reductions and other Reagan "incentives", the overall tax burden has gotten harder and pushed new people below poverty levels. The 1986 budget pushed by Reagan hits domestic issues with renewed vigor, and pulverizes the small gains of the poor into dust. The farmer is seen by the Reagan administration as being "non-competitive" in the world market, and so, to "encourage" the farmer to greater competition, Ronald Reagan proposes a five-year phasing out of operating costs and premium subsidies for the federal crop insurance program, end price supports, and devastate soil conservation—all with the intent to make "the farmer efficient." Nothing is said about the farmer who cannot find an adequate market for the fruits and vegetables and grains of his labors, nor for his cattle, sheep, and fowl which brings a meager return from the processor who in turn will charge an astronomical fee for his investment which appears in supermarkets as roasts, dressed fowl, and a plethora of produce.

Health research is to be cut to the bare bone. AIDS (Acquired Immune Deficiency Syndrome), the deadly and incurable infectious disease, is to be cut from $96 million to $86 million in 1986, giving credance to rock-star Donna Summer's homophobic outburst that AIDS "is the sin of homosexuality"—ignoring the number of heterosexuals who have it: new-borns, babies, toddlers, women, the elderly, even nuns! Sin is seen as being punished in human suffering, and therefore, by playing god, the Reagan Administration hopes to win additional support among the xenophobes in the Christian fundamentalist neo-nazi movement of the Moral Majority who would force their religious fervor down the throats of any who disagree overtly or covertly—by not worshipping or living in their manner and according to their precepts.

In line with the cuts in health research, the Reagan Administration has charted in only $11.9 billion for food stamps, in the belief that actual participants in the program will decline by 120,000 people to an estimated 20.1 million by 1986. As the Fort Worth, Texas *Star Telegram* pointed out in its lead article of 3 February 1985, the decline will not be because there will be fewer people below the poverty line, but because those who are already poor will either have exhausted their allotment for federal assistance, or who have exhausted their strength to struggle any further to obtain the most bare and base of all creature comforts. Out of necessity these poor will sacrifice not only quality nutrition and health care for any form of food, but will turn increasingly to drugs to avoid the painful reality in which they live—in constant and increasing mental anguish.

The Reagan's barbaric attitude towards health and the poor spills over even into school lunches. Concern for the dollar is more important to Ronald Reagan and his fundamental Christian supporters than is the health of children, who call in 1985 for a dragon size cutback in federal money used to subsidize the cost of meals for school children. Reagan and his supporters demand that the school lunch subsidies be trimmed to $3.4 billion—about $200 million *less* than currently being spent, in spite of the fact that the number of children in the program has increased. Furthermore not only does Ronald Reagan want to slaughter the school lunch subsidies in a major cutting effort for the poor who have in the past taken advantage of the program, but Ronald Reagan wants to do away with the program aid altogether for the children of parents in the lower middle class (which is defined as a family of four which has a total income 185% above the poverty level—or $18,870 a year).

So that the poor will have no legal recourse against the devastating Reagan program, Ronald Reagan is erasing all funding for the Legal Services Corporation which has historically provided free of charge legal aid and assistance to the poor, and has taken on cases against the federal government—especially during the Reagan debacle America languishes under. Furthermore, to be certain that the poor do not experience a true upward mobility, education is to be dramatically limited—limited by means of federal funding. Ronald Reagan demands that spending on elementary, secondary and vocational education—the education route most frequently taken by the poor who do not generally advance into the graduate arts and sciences, remain virtually at the same level in 1986 as in 1985. This means, in truth, that education is taking a backward step, for with funding frozen at the 1985 levels, and with inflation and other costs advancing, there will be no progress, fewer teachers, less building construction, fewer textbooks purchased, and many programs curtailed in scope and content or done away with altogether—especially enrichment courses. As if this were not bad enough, funding for higher education is to be slashed from $8.5 billion to $7.9 billion in 1986; federal funding for college educations—with the exception of the Guaranteed Student Loan program—are to be done away with entirely, as is the 20-year-old Job Corps program which was implemented under the Johnson Administration to prepare graduates for actual work situations and environments.

Federal funding for public broadcasting, is to

be cut. This devastating blow is unique inasmuch as the retrogressive Reagan Administration admits that the Corporation for Public Broadcasting, a private, non-profit body created by Congress to distribute federal money to 583 public television and radio stations, "is an important national resource."

But this "important national resource" is not the only tree in the forest of America's intellectual environment to be chopped down. So, too, is science. Only military research will be kept at all time highs, while energy research is to be slashed a whopping 40% (nuclear weapons research is to be ironically increased 64% - 84%! in the budget of the Department of Energy).

Even the physical environment in America is to feel the woodsman's axe, as Ronald Reagan takes a razor-sharp swing at park and refuge land acquisitions, cutting the $220 million 1985 appropriation to a scant $13 million in 1986. Funding for park police and fire rangers is also to be cut.

While the home of forest creatures is laid open to an ravishment and rape by the hardened axes of Reagan's Administration, those on retirement pensions, especially veterans, are to be tied to an increasingly cold wall of deprivation and minimum care. As physician fees are driven up by the rise of insurance rates applied to medical practioneers, increasing numbers of veterans and retired people will be faced with the unpleasant task of choosing food or health care for themselves and their loved ones.

When the choice becomes blatantly overwhelming, many will join Jeff Bolz of Omaha, Nebraska, who became a "troll"—making his life in the crude underground beneath Houston, Texas' glistening skyline, huddling beneath bridges, in tents and tunnels and open drain pipes, as recorded for posterity in an article in the *Houston Post*, Sunday, 10 February 1985. And it will hurt veterans who are already beginning to ask what is to become of them when their pensions are cut back or stopped.

The greatest tragedy about the Reagan tax program is that the President lauds it as being religiously in tune with basic Christian fundamentalism. This bastardization of Christianity is tantamount to a theocratic tyranny, and Ronald Reagan assumes the rankly offensive position of being a new Khomeini, turning the Christian bible into an American *jihad* cry. He crassly and boldly races into scriptural exegesis with total and naked ignorance, citing Luke 14:31-32 as his *raison d'etre* for prosecuting the greatest war effort in American history, yet at the same time in his overzealous defense of an bulging and unnecessarily high defense budget, this amateur theologian-king ignores two verses earlier: Luke 14:28-29. The growing arrogance of Ronald Reagan, who calls on Christian scripture to defend his undefendable war policies would in truth do better for him and for America to remember the caveat of Luke 14:28-29, for the writer of that book penned, "For which of you, intending to build a tower, does not sit down first and count the cost, to determine whether or not there is enough money to finish it? If you don't, after you have laid the foundation, you might not be able to finish it, and you will become the laughing stock of the world."

This tragedy of citing any religious writing to defend a policy foreign to the message of thinkers of peace, such as Jesus of Nazareth, is not only catapulted beyond recognition by Ronald Reagan, but transmorgified beyond mental recognition by his military brass. Bordering on blasphemy, and in total contradiction of Christian concensus in the early epigraphic writings of Christian thought, Admiral Jame D. Watkins, chief of naval operations has taken on the trappings of demigoguery and become another American ayatollah, by declaring that the death of the 241 U.S. serviceman in the Beruit bombing of 1983—which Reagan had been warned about long before the tragedy struck, but who chose to do nothing—not believing the warning, declared that the incident was brought on by "the forces of the Anti-Christ." Even more absurd and frightening is the neo-nazi cries of the chairman of the Joint Chiefs of Staff, the theologically ignorant and crassly immature General John W. Vassey, Jr., who not only goes to prayer breakfasts around the United States urging his audiences to "enlist in God's army!" (which he equates to be the American Army), but also leads chants of "Hurrah for God!"—in truth identical to the prayer call of the Iranians *"Allah Akbar"*—which we define as fanaticism.

---

[1] See my *Islam & Woman* (Dallas: Monument Press, 1985), pp. 30f.

Terrorists in Texas

Like the Nicaraguan terrorists—the rapacious Contras—filtering death and destruction to everything they oppose; like Adolf Hilter—the early twentieth century psychotic spewing havoc across the map of Europe; like James Curtis, University of Texas at Arlington student who rasorially reaches into the freedoms of others to spell out his own brand of mind control; and, like history's other tyrants who have determined to forget their own humanity and play god, the Army of God has put its match to the hopes of countless women in Texas to initially limit and then destroy their right of choice. Late Friday night, 22 February 1985, a group of hoodlums and gangster-criminals motivated by private passions incinerated the Women's Clinic of Mesquite. The fire broke out around 10:30 in that night, causing more than $1.5 million in damages to the Seville One complex located at 3230 U.S. Highway 67, near Mesquite Community Hospital, slightly north of Eastfield College on Motley Drive. The cold-blooded arsons destroyed not only the clinic but several other offices without considering the possibility that anyone was still working within the complex—so bitingly bitter was their hate of women exercising their natural rights to be free, to control their own destinies, and to determine and attend to the needs of their private bodies.

Cummins Beatty, a special agent in charge of the Dallas District of the Bureau of Alcohol, Tobacco and Firearms for the federal government, admitted there were no clues of the perpetrators, but announced the offering of a $5,000 reward for information. Half of the Dallas office (ten agents) were assigned to the case. Sunday, 24 February, fifteen more agents were called in—some from New Mexico and Oklahoma, since the wanton destruction in Mesquite was the thirty-second bombing or arson attack on women's clinics in the last three years in the United States—ten of which have not been solved.

The Mesquite Women's Clinic had been picketed by members of the radical right and by fundamentalist Christians who declared that they were led by god. One of the demonstrators against the women's clinic, a "Mr. Smith," declaring that he "spoke for god, and" was selected "by god to be the instrument of his divine will, rooting out all corruption and evil, so that women would know their place [sic] and stay subject to their men who had the power of god in the stead of god."

Bill Price, leader of the anti-choice movement in Dallas, offered a quasiapology, claiming that none of his organization's members were responsible for the disaster. He declared, "I hope and pray that the truth comes out," and swore that if it was any member of his anti-choice group, "I hope they get what's coming to them."

Little suspicion has been directed towards any of the other complex tenants, eventhough several, such as Beverly North of Head North Hair Design, were vocally opposed to the clinic's presence, and circulated a petition to have the women's group ousted from the complex, on the grounds that the clinic was bad for their business. North was concerned about her rights, but had nothing to say about the clinic's rights and the rights of its clientele.

Much of this insensitivity towards the rights of women making personal choices concerning themselves and their destiny intensified with the twelfth anniversary of the landmark Supreme Court decision *Roe vs. Wade*. This decision legalized the woman's right of choice over her own body.

The National Organization for Women (NOW) and the Religious Coalition for Abortion Rights held vigils to protest the Radical Right's move to limit the freedom of choice, and to express their indignation at the "Army of God," which clandestinely works against liberty. These anarchists, god's bullies, have vowed to destroy every woman's clinic in America, and continue to threaten the lives of practicing staff physicians. To ward off these tyrants, freedom fighters stood guard at the clinics and the homes of the physicians, pledging themselves to stand firm in the cause of justice and the right to be free from government restrictions and controls.

In spite of the Supreme Court's ruling on *Roe vs. Wade*, Texas terrorists continue to attack, lacking all moral grounds and revealing themselves as the bullies they are. They are bullies, not because of their calculated attacks on women's clinics, but their cold verbal and frightening physical attacks on women who go to the centers for counciling and/or medical attention and care. Harassment has escalated in the name of "Jesus' love"—the Bible is cited as proof of the deity's determination to stop all abortions, to curtail the freedom of choice and individuality among women, and to subject women to the will of men. This message of hate is not only preached by men who could not, at least within the contemporary range of human knowledge on the conception and formation of a zygote capable of survival and maturation in normal circumstances, popularly called an embryo, genestate—but also by women who have accepted their social conditioning of being subordinate to a man's thinking and prowess of governance. These anti-choice terrorists refer to themselves as 'sensitive' people who cannot bear the 'killing of innocent babies,' yet whose concerns with the 'sanctity of human life' throw flammable gasoline in the faces of family planning clinic personnel, fire gunshots through the living room windows of a clinic director while her children were watching television, held clinic workers hostage while their offices were sledgehammered, and arsoned and bombed 24 separate offices and clinics in 1984 alone.

In the Texas State Senate one of the very few voices of intelligent reason rose to criticize the radical right's terrorist campaign. State Senator Oscar Mauzy of Dallas openly risked his political career by criticizing the anti-choice forces of Texas who resort to violence, declaring, "For 12 years the extent of that right [to an abortion] has been tested in our courts and the Supreme Court holds fast to the principle that women have the right and freedom to make a choice. Today we repudiate those who, in their frustration to have the laws interpreted to reflect their opinions, have resorted to violence, invasion of privacy, harassment, destruction of property, intimidation and death threats. How ironic that those who advocate the right to live risk the lives of others."

Senator Mauzy, joined in his passionate plea for reason and justice by Ms. Fridrich Meg Wilson of the Texas Women's Political Caucus and Gara LaMarche of the Texas Civil Liberties Union, criticized the anti-freedom bill introduced into the Texas Senate by the leading radical right representatives: Bob McFarland of Arlington and John Sharp of Victoria. Following Hitler's policy of state opposition to abortion and the criminalization of this act of choice, these foes of liberty determined that "morality" could be publicly legislated, and that women were chips to be bartered to their capricious and inhumane whim. Nothing has been more reprehensible and vile than this piece of proposed legislation, making it law, in some cases, that a woman is to be required to report to her husband if she chooses to control her own body and its bodily functions. A classic case of class-stratification, these totalitarian authoritarians furthermore chose to write into their legislation a ban of public funding for abortions—so that only the well to do could afford a private abortion while the poor and the lower middle income women would be forced to take to the back alleys and the darkened recesses of cesspools to secure the abortion services of untrained men and women who, like drug traffickers, butcher for money—ending not only the evolution of the fetus but also costing the woman her life. Neither McFarland nor Sharp have considered their action as a step backwards in time, and neither have expressed their concern for the frustration a poor woman will feel when she is faced with the stark reality that she has no choice in the matter of securing a medically supervised and therapeutic end to an unwanted zygote-fetus. Personifying the true classic definition of fascism, being the philosophy of a government marked by stringent social and economic controls, McFarland and Sharp's legislation makes that of Mussolini's look like a humanitarian grant to the world's poor.

The City of Mesquite gave in to terrorists and terrorism on Monday, 4 March 1985, when the City Council took a first step towards banning freechoice clinics from buildings that house other businesses. More concerned with the dollar and individual economic advancement at the cost of human freedom and medical safety for the woman facing the most critical and traumatic choice in her life—whether or not to retain a zygote embryo developing fetus—the City Council, led by Mayor Pro Tem Jimmy Culver slugged through the machiavellian measure that would effectively limit the geographic location and thereby prohibit the existence of women's clinics which offer the opportunity for abortion from operating in Mesquite—making the woman who would wish to exercise her Constitutional right a victim—of the injustice of limiting her freedom—the one who gets punished while rewarding terrorist behavior. The action was a strictly political move, not a zoning problem, for the Mesquite City Council has come under increased pressure from the radical right led by the fundamentalist ministers of the town who demand that their theological interpretations be the rule for the inhabitants and citizens. Few are brave enough to stand up against these individuals who not only seek to control human thought but human action, branding their form of bitter and senseless censorship upon all who stand in their way towards making Mesquite into a narrow and debilitating theocracy.

Reactionary radicalism is not a monopoly of the Republican Party. Demigogues in the Democratic Party in Texas are thriving as well—coming out against human freedom in ways which would make any of the members of the Bundestag in the 1930s sit up with envy and in awe.

While Jan McKenna and Bob McFarland are at the forefront of the battle to destroy human freedoms in the Republican camp, they are joined by the political aspirant L.B. Kubiak of Rockdale who, like Jacob, willingly sells the robes of freedom for political gain. Nothing more sinister has come from the Texas legislature than the tyrannical testimony Kubiak penned into proposed legislation which would deny women not only the freedom of choice but strip women of any dignity that they would have as adults under current legislation. Not only does this Texas Terror L.B. Kubiak propose that all future abortions be certified as "necessary" by a physician, but would allow anyone—any person or organization regardless of their relationship to or with the woman—to file a lawsuit to block the abortion. To add further insult to justice, Kubiak—who delights in playing the role of god—demands that physicans certify only those abortions as necessary if the woman's "age and physical, emotional, pyschological and familial" situation dictates the need.

Kubiak's bill reaches far in its attempt to enchain women to the cold wall of injustice and despocy, permitting "any injured party" to protest against her freedom of choice and the selection of the option of a therapeutic abortion. The revised measure defines an "injured party" as any family member or any organization opposed to abortion and grants them the power of being judge and executioner over the woman's fundamental human rights by filing a time-delaying lawsuit for an injunction to stop the abortion.

The tragedy of the politics of L.B. Kubiak is that when he introduced his measure, he labeled it as a marginal deterrent to late abortions—those coming in the 25th to 27th week. His disguise off, Kubiak revealed his true barbaric plans, which made Sheila Cheaney and Pam Fridrich denounce the crass and self-gratifying legislator as misrepresenting himself and his bill during a committee hearing the third week of April, 1985. His demonic demonstration of lack of human compassion and feeling was championed by the self-serving State senator from Victoria, John Sharp, another Democrat whose own political aspirations override any interest in the democratic process. To win the support for further political advance, they like McKenna and McFarland preach the glories of "The Silent Scream" which details the alleged pain of an unborn zygote, while never even mentioning the pain, agony, and heartbreak of the woman who must make a choice, and instead of attempting to abort the unwanted fetus with a closet clothes hanger or seeking release of the unwanted object turns to back alley butchers.

The Radical Right, led by Jan McKenna, Bob McFarland and Jim Norwood of Arlington continue to work against human freedom and the right of choice by campaigning to limit a woman's control over her body's destiny, by means of showing a fraudulent and emotionally exploitative film entitled *The Silent Scream.* Despite the fact that leading medical authorities have labeled the film's message as "erroneous" and "ridiculous," it is pushed by this anti-democratic trio since it was endorsed by Ronald Reagan and the White House, inflaming the builders of bombs, arsonists who claim they act for god, and tyrants like James Curtis who demand that their brand of morality be the official code of the community.

The *Silent Scream*, a 28-minute film that allegedly records the sensational portrayal of the abortion of a 12-week-old fetus is narrated by Dr. Bernard Nathanson who freezes the ultrasound picture and points to the apparently open mouth of the fetus as the suction device to achieve the abortion is inserted into the womb. A former abortion clinic director and now anti-choice crusader, Dr. Nathanson has emotionally declared that he conceived of making the film when he heard Ronald Reagan—who has no medical credentials whatsoever—say fetuses feel "long and agonizing pain" during an abortion. Reagan's statement has no foundation in fact, nor is he or his argument recognized by the medical community as being sound, well researched and demonstratively provable.

The errors and distortions of *The Silent Scream* are as numerous as the illogical, irrational and politically controversial statements and questionable to out-right false medical assertions presented in this highly emotional, factually inaccurate, anti-choice polemic. Among those which are the most reprehensible in this flight of fancy and escape from reality, a testimony to Hollywood at its very worse, are three: the claims that neither the medical practioneers performing therapeutic abortions nor the women knew much about the fetus; that a fetus is the same as a child and can feel, think, react and exhibit purposeful activity; and that it is not necessary to include women's experiences in a discussion of abortion. The chauvinism of the film is best illustrated by its own denial of women the right to speak at any time during the presentation. Instead the women pictured are shown as either pregnant and smiling, prone during an abortion, or crying because they somehow made a "mistake" in seeking to exercise their Constitutional guaranteed right of freedom of choice and securing an abortion.

A major injustice to truth and scientific reality came in the actual filming of the polemic, for a late-term fetus is shown first on a sonogram while a twelve-week-old fetus is not. That was done deliberately since the producers knew that a fetus is not distinguishable during its first twelve weeks while it is in the last stage of evolution. Furthermore, a doll was placed directly under the screen of the sonogram to suggest that the fetus is a baby—which it is not. It would have been far more authentic and factual if the film producers of this big money-making commerically inspired and sold movie had placed a model of a twelve week fetus under the screen and shown that there is little to distinguish it from the fetus of any other mammal.

At best *The Silent Scream* is medical chicanery, as confirmed by Dr. Pasko Rakic in *The New York Times* of 25 January 1985, *Philadelphia Inquirer* of 27 January 1985, and *Washington Post* of 9 February 1985. Rejecting the film as unscientific and filled with numerous distortions of fact, the Chair of neuroanatomy at the Yale University School of Medicine details that a fetus in the first twelve weeks attempting to escape an abortion instrument "is like saying a ping pong ball moves when you put it in a bowl of water and stir it with a pencil." Furthermore, as for the contention that the fetus "screams", "in order to scream one would have to have synapses of the cortex," which a fetus before the last months does not have. Dr. Edwin C. Meyer, chair of the department of pediatric neurology of the Medical College of Virginia in Richmond concurred, saying, "To make a statement that a fetus feels pain is a totally ridiculous statement. Pain implies cognition. There is no brain to receive the information." (*New York Times* 25 January 1985). His judgement was endorsed and supported by the Chair of pediatric neurology at New York Hospital at Cornell Medical Center in New York, who affirmed "The notion that a 12-week fetus screams in discomfort is erroneous." But demigogues who are determined to control the destiny of women and destroy their freedom of choice glory in the destruction of truth and the presentation of half-truths and lies to further their draconic designs.

   The film misleads the viewers. At best the fetus is a clump of cells which can neither writhe or scream with pain, as was pointed out by Dr. Marvin Frishcman, director of pediatric neurology at Baylor College of Medicine in Houston—who has seen the film. Frischman defended his analysis against the condemnation of the vocal anti-choice movement in Texas by detailing that to experience the pain as is suggested by Dr. Nathanson, a fetus would need a relatively mature nervous system capable of carrying pain impulses from the body to the brain. Such a system would need two working parts: well-formed nerve fibers to transmit the pain impulses along the spinal cord to the brain and chemical neurotransmitters capable of carrying the signal from neuron to neuron. A fetus in the twelfth week has neither of these prerequisites, as neural pathways do not mature enough to transmit pain impulses until mid-pregnancy or later, and, as Frischman said, "certainly not before the [end of the] first trimester."

The fact is that the fetus does not produce the chemicals necessary to experience pain until the last three months of the pregnancy. Thus what *The Silent Scream* shows is not a scream of pain, but rather a reflex commonly seen in lower animals and humans with undeveloped brains. Nathanson's arguments, therefore, are neurophysiologically inaccurate. The director of neurology at Southwestern Medical School in Dallas, Dr. Roger Rosenberg—who says he is anti-abortion, condemns the film, claiming that the suggestion of a scream is "a gross extrapolation."

The volatile nature of the film has encouraged a wave of violence which Jerry Falwell and other members of the affluent radical right Moral Majority corporation have endorsed by affirming their willingness to pay the legal expenses of American terrorists who transmorgify the laws of America by bombing women's centers and attempting to murder physicians who support the American Constitutional guarantee of freedom of choice. Vulnerable and uninformed individuals are frequently fooled by the irrational and medically unsubstantiated claims of the movie and commit themselves to the support or actual involvement in new terorist crime waves.

The arrogance of the anti-choice forces and the growing number of terrorists masquerading as being the "Army of God," grew in the opening statements of T. Patrick Monaghan, a lawyer from Bardstown, Kentucky, given at the Pensacola, Florida trial of four young demigogues who bombed women's clinics on Christmas Day. Lauding the terrorist quartet as "knights in shining armor," Monaghan cited alleged popular support for their atrocities committed not only against freedom but against the people who had placed their trust in a government which promised them protection, "life, liberty and the pursuit of happiness."

While Jerry Falwell promised to pay the legal expenses of America's religious fanatics who demonstrate their opposition to choice by means of arson and other forms of terrorism, thereby giving his tacit blessing to their program for dismantling American democracy and the principles of freedom of choice, Assistant U.S. Attorney Susan Novotny told the jury that Matthew Goldsby, James Simmons, Kathren Simmons and Kaye Wiggins were criminals who conducted "very intricate and very well-planned" attacks on a clinic and the offices of two doctors where abortions were performed. Her words were not encouraging to the Texas terrorists who look to the courts for acquital and vindication of their heinous and cold-blooded assaults on the very foundation of American democracy.

In part this fear was generated when one jurist, State District Judge Peter Michael Curry of San Antonio dissolved a temporary restraining order which cleared the path for a 19-year-old woman to have an abortion, on Wednesday, 28 March 1985. His action undid the restraining order placed against Kim Hayes the previous week at the request of her estranged husband, Keith, who claimed that he should be able to veto the woman's freedom of choice. Although Judge Curry affirmed his personal opposition to abortion, he detailed his positive stand in permitting the woman freedom of choice, declaring soundly, "I'm a believer in the Constitution of the United States. I can't see how I have the right to prevent this lady from having an abortion."

The tragedy of *Silent Scream* is it not only frightens but torments hundreds of women facing a most difficult choice. At the same time it makes a mockery of the American commitment to individual freedom as guaranteed in the United States Constitution and upheld by the United States Supreme Court in the landmark decision *Roe vs. Wade.*

Jerry Falwell, who drives luxury cars while the poor of Virginia walk, recklessly races his riding mower in the direction of his gardener, and encourages his son to dress and mingle among the same homosexuals he condemns, continues to perpetuate the cruel and unfortunate hoax that women turn to abortion as a matter of "convenience"—without realizing that less than a half a generation ago women could terminate a pregnancy in America only with the risk of pain, injury, and even death—without benefit of anesthesia or sanitary conditions. Women literally had abortions in back alleys or on kitchen tables if they did not attempt to self-abort by using coat hangers, knitting needles, and lye douches.

Intimidation and intolerance of the Radical Right who cover their attempts to establish a religious inquisition in America and destroy the freedom of choice flourishes as long as people remain silent. Anti-choice forces led by Ronald Reagan continue to harass freedom fighters while Republican Senators Gordon Humphrey of New Hampshire and Jesse Helms of North Carolina introduce into the Senate the "Civil Rights Act for the Unborn," that declares a "sense of the Senate" that the fetus feels pain. Such actions conveys remarkable arrogance and defies all verifiable scientific evidence. Furthermore, it indicates unspeakable disdain for women, who don't need the "sense of the Senate" to tell them that they feel pain. Women know that!

Linda Hosek reported for the Fort Worth *Star Telegram* (29 May 1985, 2A) that David Norman's mother presented him a cake decorated with a skull and crossbones, symbol of the Legion of Doom, on his 18th birthday, at a party of hot dogs and balloons with 'Legion of Doom' on them. Neighbor Phyllis VanAllen called it an "all-American picture."

David Norman, of 2919 Alton Road, is reported to have exclaimed in aspiration, "I want to be either the richest man or president or king of the western empire." Judy Norman, the boy's mother, admitted that she was concerned about her son's prejudices and lack of compassion, but said she was proud of his willingness to be a "leader."

A special investigative police force in Fort Worth, Texas submitted evidence to a grand jury on 19 April 1985 that no less than eight Paschall High School students were involved and engaged in organized criminal activity with the intent to do great bodily harm and injury to property. The grand jury returned indictments on specific acts rather than on the overall criminal conspiracy and organized crime of Paschall High School students David "Beaver" Norman, 18.

Neo-Nazism
and the Legion of Doom
of Fort Worth

While most of the world is recovering from the barbaric and wanton destruction of the holocaust launched by the maniac Adolf Hitler in the first half of the twentieth century, slaughtering over six million innocent peoples, destroying ethnic treasures, and making a general mockery out of justice, democracy and human compassion, a few select individuals from R.L. Paschall High School in Fort Worth are rekindling the fires of hatred, bigotry, violence and murder in the cause of self-gratification, self awareness and self advancement: the true image of the Yuppies of the 1980s. These are not unlettered, disenfranchised or poor people, but spring from the stagnant cistern of wealth, education and privilege, for one of the storm troopers of the Legion of Doom is an honor student, another a cheerleader for the Panthers, and yet another a husky football player—all of who receive above average academic scores, are involved in school activities, and have won peer respect. They are joined by a contender for the position of class valedictorian, a pre-med and a pre-law student—all who hold, like Sid Fitzwater, the thesis that their interpretation of the law and the benefits and protection of the law is correct, infallible, and solitary. Together these students, along with at least four others, have formed a special and illegal vigilante group which randomly and irrationally conducts violence, engages in harassement, and promises other forms of retribution against those who they feel endangered by. All of the members were, originally, hall monitors at the school.

Insecure in their own sexual identity, the Legion of Doom first harassed homosexuals. Uncertain of their own sexual orientation and affectional interests, the Legion of Doom felt that by attacking homosexuals the members were demonstrating their avid and zealous pro-Republican Party support. These demigogues tyrannized anyone they suspected of being homosexual. When questioned by the local police, they admitted their homophobia, excusing it by claiming that "by driving through fag park" (Forest Park—about eight blocks from Paschall High School), and harassing people they thought were gay, they found "an innocent way to amuse" themselves, the Arlington *Daily News* reported 1 April 1985..

Their activities have included car demolition by means of a pipe bomb, leaving threatening notes embellished with swastikas on the desks of students they oppose, and occasionally tossing a deliberately slain cat into a student's car. Another cat was dissected and its blood was smeared on the paint and upholstery of a victim's car.

According to Fort Worth Police spokesperson Doug Clarke, more than thirty crimes have been committed in the name of "purifying society" by these neo-Nazis. The majority of these incidents were felonies, all done with a Yuppie psychology and crass disinterest in the civil rights of others.

The Legion of Doom is composed of young people. Their ages range from 16 to 19. They are all honor students from "good families" of substantial financial means. They are top athletes and are involved in student government. Their heroes include Jerry Falwell and Phyllis Schlafly. They oppose the intermingling of races and lifestyles. Far right in political philosophy, they are equally radical in religious "orthodoxy." They demand *their* censorship in areas of movies, books, magazines, and other means of human expression. Their thesis is to "clean up the school." Since they feel that they cannot work "within the system" they have taken the cloak of godheadship upon themselves and have become the new tyrants, stressing that their actions were the result of things happening in Paschal High that couldn't be taken care of through "the system." To this end they made weapons, including a homemade rocket launcher—for they believe their way to be right even if their judgement brings about Armageddon, whole sale slaughter, or even their own death. They are as firmly committed to their cause as were Joseph Paul Goebbels and the SS elite forces of Nazi Germany. As the Fort Worth Police have determined, nearly all of the

Bradley James Bielss

members of this neo-Nazi movement are white males who have a definite racist and anti-Semetic philosophy and stand. "They plan on killing all Jews and blacks," one Paschal High School senior confessed. A junior, who would allow himself to be identified only as "Rick," declared, "They're prejudiced, and they think like Hitler. They want to be supreme." Another junior, "Mary," detailed further, "They want to take over the school. Some even say they want to take over Fort Worth and Texas. Then they mean to clear out all gays, blacks, Jews, and Mexicans. They want a religious society that follows the Bible. One claims that this will only be done when [Jerry] Falwell is elected President and the Moral Majority stoke up the fires to burn the non-believers."

During the second week of April, 1985, Bradley James Bielss, believed by the Fort Worth Police to be one of the ten members of the Legion of Doom at Paschal High School of Fort Worth, was suspended from school for, allegedly, showing a

---

The similarity between the neo-Nazi movement in the United States and the Legion of Doom at Paschall High School in Fort Worth cannot be ignored or discounted. "The Order"—a violent arm of the American Nazi party has bombed a synagogue in Boise, Idaho. The Legion of Doom has pipe bombed a Paschall High School student's car. "The Order" has murdered a man they considered "socially unacceptable" in Denver. The Paschall High School athletic honor students who make up the Legion of Doom have threated to kill those who do not conform to their self-anointed standards of personal conduct. The American Nazis are anti-Semitic, anti-Black, homophobic, and swear to force a religious conservativism upon America after they take over the United States in an armed revolution; their spokesperson is an ordained fundamentalist minister, Richard Girnt Butler, who heads the Aryan Nations, the white supremacy organization located in Hayden Lake which has spawned several of The Order's founders. The Fort Worth Legion of Doom vows are similar, and swear their allegiance to fundamentalist Baptist television evangelist Jerry Falwell who is committed to paying the legal fees of American terrorists, has laid out a blue print for the take over of American in his *Moral Majority Report* (see my *Idol Worshippers in Twentieth Century America*), and has proclaimed that he will see

handgun to coach and social studies instructor James Crowder on the school grounds. Crowder was suspended from his coaching duties because he failed to report the incident. He was allowed to continue to teach his academic courses. Bielss, a senior, was scheduled to graduate—before the incident. When he was suspended his parents filed

---

public education erased from America, and all classes taught strictly by fundamentalist Christians. The crimes of the American Nazis range from extortion to murder—charges so serious that the Federal Bureau of Investigation has arrested more than 20 people since November 1984, including several charged with being accessories after the fact or with harboring members of The Order. The Fort Worth Police are continuing their investigations of the honor students who make up the radical Legion of Doom, have brought charges against most who have been linked to bombings, threats, and similar terrorist tactics. The name of the Legion of Doom of Fort Worth appears on the bulletins of the American Nazi Party, and the American Nazi Party's right wing The Order issued in Fall of 1984 a thirteen page manifesto proclaiming war against the United States and Canada, promising to kill all politicians, judges, journalists, bankers, soldiers, and police officers as well as federal agents who got in their way of "purifying" the American society by liquidating Jews, Blacks, Gays, and other minorities they feel threatened by due to their own uncertainty as to their sexual and psycho-physiological identifications. The same uncertainty over sexual identification and proclivity understanding plagues the members of the Legion of Doom as demonstrated in their attacks on any member who does not appear to have or express the same sexual mannerism and interests as the strict fundamentalist radical right in American declare is "normal". In both cases, as in other cases concerning American terrorists, they are championed and defended by alleged "ministers of god"—the 66-year-old Butler defending the American Nazis who argued that "they were pushed to the wall. They had no future. If you're white and declare yourself white, you're ostracized by this Jewish-controlled [sic] society. You can't get a job. You're a non-entity."

"When this happens to virile, white men...they react." Butler prophecied: "You're going to see more of that [violence and armed revolution]." At the same time the defenders of the Legion of Doom argue that the crimes committed by the calloused crusaders were "the sport of kids".

In both cases concerning these American terrorists is that they attempt to excuse their atrocities on the spurious grounds that their revolution is based on biblical premises purportedly endorsing religious and racial and even sexual superiority. The seriousness of their threat is in terms of their capability to use violence, to attack Blacks, Jews, Gays, and any other person or group of people who does not conform to their rigid standards. They are engaged in a serious business—and they mask it behind the altar of religion. Religion has cloaked the evil machinations of those who would destroy the Constitution.

suit seeking his reinstatement so that he could take the exams needed for graduation. The suspension was an automatic result of current school and district policy which prohibits students from bringing weapons to the school. The suspension is for the term of the academic year.

The greatest tragedy of the radical far-right in America is the growing interest possession and use of guns. Bradley James Bielss believed it was his right to carry a gun to Paschall High School and show it to varsity baseball coach Jimmie Crowder with the same fervor and zeal as neo-Nazi David Lane (suspect as a member of the four-man hit squad in the murder of Jewish Denver talk-host Alan Berg, an outspoken foe of anti-Semitism and frequently argued with neo-Nazis on his call-in show, shooting the celebrity in the driveway of his home on 18 June 1984) took a .45 caliber pistol and a large knife to a supermarket parking lot in Winston-Salem, North Carolina. Lane was intimate with members of the Ku Klux Klan at the time of his arrest, and vowed that a revolution would sweep American Jewry, Blacks, Gays, and "militant women" into the sea.

In each case where violence has occurred, and where the individual responsible for the terrorism that was launched was taken into custody, the common defense has been that it was that individual's right to "save" America from "the enemy". The "enemy" was any one who had a different view point or means of expression opposite or not in line with that view point of means of expression held and expounded by the terrorist. Thus the Legion of Doom of Fort Worth issued threatening notes, emblazoned swastikas on the notes and elsewhere, and exploded cars, killed animals which were used as warnings to unpopular students, and committed over twenty other forms of terrorist acts with the intent of limiting other individuals constitutionally guaranteed rights to liberty, life and the pursuit of happiness.

All of the protestations of Attorney Tom Zachry, representing two of the alleged members of the Legion of Doom, that "this thing has gotten totally out of hand. I don't think there's any major philosophy of Nazism involved. Swastikas are the kind of typical things kids will write anywhere in the world" (Dallas *Times Herald*, 18 April 1985, p. A-32) is at best wishful thinking, and at worse is a gross misunderstanding of the *modus operandi* of youth and a statement emasculating the basic sense of right youth has. The atrocities of the Nazis, although dim in many minds, remains vivid to the educated—which is what, supposedly, the members of the Legion of Doom are. Their actions are inexcusable.

While attorneys David Lobingier and Paul Connor argue that there is no connection between the Legion of Doom and the American Nazi Party, it is difficult to explain, if their judgement is correct, how the name of the Legion got to the Nazi The Order, and why the Legion of Doom's name as a group appears on The Order's bulletin board.

Students who are friends with the members of the Legion of Doom (the legion members actually call themselves the "Lejun uf Dume") testify that the legionnaires are "a right-wing supremacy group." One 18 year old, who gave a statement to the Fort Worth Police, affirmed that the Legion was originally patterned after the fictional "Super Friends" cartoon show carried on television.

Like all demigogues they justify their actions: claiming that the violence they engage is only a mirror of divine retribution in their crusade to rid the school and society of "dopers, thieves, kids who were assaulting teachers." The extent of their commitment to the Nazi philosophy, policy, pogrom and practice is dramatically demonstrated in the note they left on the windshield of one student's car that read: "Paschall is now Nazi territory. You are short-lived if you return. Heed our warning, there will not be another." Another note, found with a swastika, by a car that was bombed, read: "We do not like thieves. This is your last warning," and implied that if the sixteen year old owner did not perform in the manner which they believed was correct and to them acceptable, he would be eliminated "as a trouble maker."

The violence of the Legion of Doom began one day when the members went to a McDonald's fast food emporium to "hose down everyone with a fire hose." Their victims were fellow students who did not rigidly hold to their radical rightist ideas. From that point on, the serpentine senselessness of violence intensified and increased, especially after one of their members obtained a copy of *The Anarchists Cookbook* (which contains instructions on how to make bombs at home). They immediately began applying the "recipes" and creating their own arsenal "to take over the school".[1]

The fact is that the Legion of Doom wants to do more than "take over the school." Members have taken it upon themselves to "clean up the community."

Bob Whitehead of Fort Worth had his porch light shot out by an M-1 carbine, on Sunday, 22 March 1985. This was not an initial attack. Two months earlier his stepson had the windows of his Mustang smashed while it was parked outside the family home. Earlier several nuts from the front wheel had been removed—because the youth had dated a girlfriend of one of the gang's members.

By 29 March 1985, new allegations surfaced, bringing a Tarrant County Junior College student into the list of those who used swastikas to mark their victims and their deeds. All the police would say, at that time, is the new evidence is "very serious in nature." Some Tarrant County Junior College students hypothesize that it includes death threats, and attempts to solicit murder of the more liberal members of the college community and Fort Worth in general.

By the middle of April, 1985, the Fort Worth Police were investigating whether or not the Legion of Doom was connected with the violent splinter group of Aryan Nations—a neo-Nazi organization headquartered in Idaho now under in-

---

[1]Margaret Scott, " 'Good kids' suspected in vigilante violence," Dallas *Times Herald* (26 March 1985) pp. 1, 20. Cf. " 'Legion of Doom' called bullies," Arlington *Daily News* (29 March 1985) 6-A. Interviews conducted with students by the author.

vestigation by federal authorities. Interest in the possibility of the connection was sparked when federal investigators found the name and mention of the Legion of Doom on a national computer bulletin board used by the Ayran Nations splinter group The Order which has been active in El Paso.

America's Nazi Party recognizes the Legion of Doom as a co-equal: the same in political and social ideology, and willing to take all risks and use any measure to further its totalitarian and freedom limiting goals—using terror to push its plans for a revitalized slave state in Texas where those who are to be enchained are those people the Legion of Doom considers unworthy for life.

The fear of the rise of a new Nazi movement in America is very real. By 1985 the neo-Nazi movement in America has claimed the responsibilities for several arsons, bombings and murders, including the senseless slaying of a Denver radio personality, and the wanton execution of a Missouri state trooper, allegedly gunned down by fugitive construction worker David C. Tate, age 22, of Athol, Idaho. Tate was one of 24 members of the Ayran Nations Idaho unit, and a companion and colleague of William Anthony Nash, who was arrested in Philadelphia on Wednesday, 18 April 1985, on the charge of continuing criminal offenses. What makes this neo-Nazi coterie most frightening is the chilling reality that nearly all of its members are young: under 30 years of age, with the median age in the early 20s; all are supporters of the radical right movement in politics and in religion, deploring any form of deviance from the status quo as determined by such fundamentalists as the former Congressional representatives McDonald of Georgia and Hall of Rockwall, Texas; are ardent supporters of the privilege of carrying weapons, which are shown to colleagues in testimony of their virility and determination to clean up America; and expound the principle of "cleaning up America" of drug traffickers, "wet-backs and niggers," homosexuals, and all others who counter their plan for a "pure America." The Legion of Doom has endorsed all of these goals and has adopted the same as its organizational credo.

CHARLES FILLMORE   DAVID NORMAN   JOE DORRIS

On Tuesday, 28 May 1985, eight members of the self-styled vigilante terrorist group known as the Legion of Doom were charged in 33 indictments for criminal acts ranging from manufacturing a Molotov cocktail to the pipe bombing of a car. Sons of privilege, the indicted neo-Nazis of Fort Worth included Paschall High School senior David Norman (age 18, charged with three felonies and four misdemeanors, for which, if Norman is convicted could bring him a maximum penalty of 53 years in prison and a $30,000 fine). He was voted "most popular student". Indictments were also handed down against James Bradley Bielss (age 18, charged with reckless conduct and criminal mischief), Charles W. Fillmore (age 18, charged with aggravated assault, criminal mischief, and possession of a prohibited weapon), Joe David Dorris (age 17, charged with arson, possession of a prohibited weapon, and criminal mischief), James A. Turner (age 17, charged with arson, possession of a prohibited weapon and criminal mischief), Dareen K. Deitrich (age 17, charged with possession of a prohibited weapon and aggravated assault, and criminal mischief), Michael Taw Guthrie (age 17, charged with possession of a prohibited weapon, and aggravated assault), and James Harrison Mathis, Jr. (age 18, charged with possession of a prohibited weapon)—the fact that weapons were involved should delight Texas legislator J.E. Brown of Lake Jackson who successfully pushed through a law prohibiting cities from regulating guns.

Kent Hance:
Political Opportunist

Amorality a confession of political expediency, Dimmit, Texas native Kent Hance has pulled out all stops in his golliwog grasping climb to power and prestige, making Texas a golgatha for its people. Lacking all principles and strength to be a person of his word, Hance willingly sells his rhetoric and service to the highest bidder. Whereas in April of 1985 this chalcidic chameleon cavorts capriciously and, like ancient Essau, trades his patrimony and heritage for the bowl of pottage that the Republican radical rights offers to him with blood-stained hands—milking the life work and trust of the poor, the downtrodden, the helpless and friendless for the pleasure of the wealthy who dance on the grave site of democracy.

A graduate from Texas Tech University in 1965, and University of Texas Law School in 1968, Kent Hance began his McCarthyist climb towards limiting human freedom and speaking out in defense of the greed of the insensitive rich after serving as a professor of business law at Texas Tech from 1968-1974. At the age of 31 Hance was elected to the Texas Senate in 1974, and served on the Finance and State Affairs Committee without distinction in the areas of human concerns. Defeating Vice President George Bush's son, George W. Bush, Jr., in 1978, Hance went on to Congress where he began laying the ground work for the mausoleum in which he would lay the the ignored, the homeless, the victims of rape and the forgotten farmers. His legislation helped to write the Reagan Administration's book shutting off the channels to justice and equal opportunity to the lower and middle class American so that rich corporations and individuals would pay less tax or none at all, funding terrorist movements either directly or through the political action corporation Moral Majority Inc which thrives on issuing a menacing message of hate and bigorty in its sericeous selachian pulp *Moral Majority Report..* Together with those who would destroy democracy, Kent Hance stands behind the greedy.

Consciously anti-Black, anti-woman, anti-gay, anti-choice, anti-human freedom and against equal opportunity supported by mandate and federal law, Kent Hance declared in April 1985 that he had "no plans to change parties or wives," gave the continuing lie to his declarations by joining the Republican Party on Friday, 3 May 1985—entering the fold he intellectually and philosophically had always been a member and affirmant He has not yet informed the voters of Texas when he will introduce the next Mrs. Hance to campaign beside him.

As the Dallas *Times Herald* of 3 May 1985 (16-A) noted, a good part of Hance's timing on switching officially to the Republican Party came when he was warned by wealthy Republican contributors that "It's now or never—you're losing valuable time." if he wanted to cash in on the bulging Republican political war chest of funds and supporters. These funds would be essential to Hance if he finalized his decision to run against either moderate-to-conservative Democrat Governor Mark White, or against conservative-to-ultraconservative Democrat Senator Lloyd Bensten.

Hance had declared in San Francisco during the Democratic Convention of 1984 that he would remain a Democrat "regardless of pressure" to switch his party affiliation. He stood at the convention extolling the virtues of the Democratic Party, and affirmed his lifelong commitment to it. His rejection of his affirmation gives credence to the judgement of State Senator Lloyd Doggett, who referred to Hance as "an opportunist."

While a sizeable majority of his constituents were shocked at Hance's defection, the greatest shock appeared among his strongest supporters, including State Representative Mark Stiles of Beaumont who hinted broadly that he felt "betrayed". Stiles summed up the popular sentiment when he declared, "I don't know what he's [Hance] running for, but if I was him, I'd be running for the state line."

Kent Hance

A man whose word cannot be trusted or statements taken for granted, a man whose credibility does not exist and whose posturings bid only disbelief, Kent Hance's switch to the

Republican Party demonstrates the extent of his commitment to personal ambitions and vested petty interests; his willingness to sell his ideals and his voice for personal political aspirations, aligned with his need to feel a part of the "in-crowd," regardless of any values he had declared earlier in his career. Willing to prejudice any effort he allegedly supports, and to sell out those who came to him—seeking him as their champion—Kent Hance has willed a death call to freedom and objectivity in Texas, as can be seen in the "white oil" bill he placed in jeopardy after affirming his willingess to stand firm for the principles he declared were sacred and inviolable.

Texas citizens can only have serious concerns over an individual who says one thing one day and then summarily rejects the same personal credo and adopts its antithesis the next. Kent Hance took away the faith and hope of thousands of supporters who had believed him, in error, to be an honorable man of dignity, resolve, and purpose—as testified to by Pampa attorney Miles O'Laughlin, chairperson of the trade organization TEAM that represents independent oil and gas producers in five Panhandle counties.

Rather than being the anticipated "role model" for future generations of Texans, Hance has put himself into becoming the antithesis of responsibility and integrity. Looming large on the horizon of the future is the inevitability of his selling off his commitment to offer a viable alternative in the political process by abandoning hope in the reality of change. Instead of working towards adding a strong conservative voice to the Democratic Party, he has fled in personal fear that

America is not able to afford dissenting opinions in both political parties.

This demigogue has taken up the imperial and stagnant ideas of the Watergate era, pulsing with Nixon in his disinterest in common labor for a unified nation. Offering an end to prosperity and peace as the 1980s hoped for, Kent Hance stands as standard bearer of the promise for nuclear holocaust and the pestilence of Armaggedon by urging war as an instrument to insure peace, by the waste of natural resources for immediate profit, and by the nuclear proliferation of untested, overpriced, and poorly constructed weapons, whose only benefit will be to make the rich richer.

In reality a racist who condemns not only black American citizens but other near-voiceless minorities ranging from women to gays, Kent Hance promises the continued division of America along racist lines—in keeping with the program of the radical right that has a strangle hold upon the Republican Party. As seen in the racially polarized vote in the 1984 presidential elections in America, Kent Hance promises to be a driving and divisive force behind partisan realignment in Texas, giving strength to those who would be gods, regardless if they wear the hooded white robes of the Ku Klux Klan, or are members of the neo-Nazi movement the Legion of Doom, or march with Intelivote and conservative ministers who bastardize the gospel in a thinly veiled threat to human dignity and democracy. He lusts after the governorship and will not be stopped by principles or scruples. His word is nothing.

Miracle Sunday

EVERYONE BRING ONE

PASTOR LARRY LEA

Church on the Rock
Sunday May 5th, 10:00 am.
Dallas Convention Center Aud.

SPECIAL GUESTS
EVANGELIST
JAMES ROBISON
AND
GRAMMY AWARD WINNER
RUSS TAFF

TEXAS
C·U·THR

Religious Fanaticism in Texas

There is a growing tide of religious radicalism racing across the plains of Texas. It is appearing in cosmopolitan and rural areas. It is strangling freedom of thought, choice, and consentual action in a plethora of areas ranging from worship to marital relationships and socio-economic lifestyles. It is interfering with due process of government, jurisprudence, and justice—all in the hypocritic name of faith, where it is more important to affirm the confessions of a self-styled high priest that it has not only canonized, but deified as well.

No longer believing in the principles of the separation of church and state, the religious right is openly working for a theocracy in America. It's goals is to weed-out and destroy those who do not agree with it. It's adherents come from such well-known and all encompassing fascist groups such as the Moral Majority, to the lesser known organizations who label themselves as "Political Action Committees" who would homogenize society beyond even the most rigid totalitarian's wildest fantasies. Among these groups, Intelivote Network stands out in rigid righteousness—like the Sanhedrin of ancient Israel which sat in judgement not only of ontological orthodoxy, but personal expression, life patterns and interpersonal relationships.

Raising thousands of dollars for the purpose of getting "acceptable" candidates elected to public office, it sends out questionnaires to imcumbents and aspiring political candidates. The questionnaires do not address the political philosophies and programs of the candidates, but instead demand to know the candidates most intimate secrets. From what information is given them, Intelivote Network rates and ranks candidates on the basis of thier morality, character, and citizenship—to the second decimal point.

Geared to mind control, this fascist organization was started in Mesquite, Texas during the first quarter of 1985. It's executive director is Wyatt W. Lipscomb, a Garland lawyer. Over 100 ministers and lay people attended the meeting, with the pastor of the First Assembly of God in Mesquite, Rev. Norton Richardson, heading the assault on the existing separation of church and state. Mesquite ministers urged their flock to call on their co-parishioners to vote as Christian legalistic Sadduccees, rigidly holding to the literal words of a book printed in English as if the original authors knew the language and the customs of twentieth century Texas.

Within a month, from 25 February to 26 March these menacing Mesquite ministers, cloaking their theocratic aspiration under the guise of being civic minded, gathered more than $4,450. Nineteen people, all from Mesquite, contributed more than $50, feeling that they have the right to impose their religion on those who do not share it nor wish to embrace it and its principles. At the top of the Intelivote Network is the goal to continue to refuse basic human civil rights for homosexuals, and to deny women the Constitutional guaranteed freedom of choice concerning the governance of her own body. Commited to a policy against freedom of choice, the anti-choice forces of the Intelivote Network have interrogated candidates in local elections as to their stand on abortion and human rights. Those candidates which affirmed the basic principles of the Constitution of the United States, guaranteeing the individual citizen the right to the pursuit of individual happiness in the area of choice of self-governance and personal affectional expression, have been blasted as being against the popular will with the implication that they are serving as anti-Christs.

In the despotic queue of religious intolerance stands Rev. Don Bradley of the First Baptist Church of Mesquite. He has confirmed to the news media that his paramount mission is to discover how candidates in the Mesquite election stand on "certain moral questions." Bradley intends to distribute the findings to his docile congregation, as if he were Caiaphas pronouncing sentence on the actions of the civil leaders, urging those who do not meet his standards to be stoned by ballots poised against them like large rocks ready to slice open their minds and drain from their skulls all vistages of independent thought and philosophic analysis.

Intelivote has no interest in tolerance—as Christ preached, but instead has determined that it is better than Christ and can judge others more soundly, correctly and completely than can even their god (cf. Matt. 7:1, Acts 10:24). Intelivote, like the minions Bradley and Richardson, refuse to recognize the basic fact in life that discrimination in any form is inconsistent with both the bible and the American Constitution. Instead, as their plan is laid out, one can speculate that their chief interest is to restore the intolerance of Calvin's sixteenth century Geneva, and burn heretics on the fires of their scourging denunciations and moves to depose those who disagree.

In spite of Intelivote's drive to oust those political candidates which scored low on their "morality scale," the majority survived, including Mesquite Mayor Brunhilde Nystrom, a Methodist, who received a rating of 4.73 on a scale of 1 to 15. Ms. Nystrom's low score was the result of her refusal to answer questions about her views on such irrelevant issues as restricting "pornography," abortion, and the hiring of homosexuals as city employees. Her objections, she stated, to answering such tyrannically freedom-limiting questions as those posed to her by Intelivote, was because a conservative church group's rating of candidates on moral and religious issues made the town look "stupid and backward."

Mayor Brunhilde Nystrom
Refuses to capitulate to the 1985 Mesquite Intelivote political fulminations

The fulminations and attempts to control politics by Intelivote were not restricted exclusively to the city of Mesquite. Those who would determine public policy, making up the storm troopers of the Intelivote gang, penetrated Arlington and surrounding towns as well. As the Arlington *Daily News* (17 April 1985, pp. 1A, 6A) reported, Intelivote questioned several Arlington City Council members concerning their personal religious beliefs and affirmations, on which they "graded" the candidates from "A" to "D"—with two of the candidates failing, receiving no grade at all.

Misrepresenting themselves as citizens of Arlington, Intelivote gave Jen Barney a "D"—even though she refused to answer any questions from the group. Councilwoman Dottie Lynn was the most upset, and issued the strongest statement againt the gestapo tactics of the radical fringe group Intelivote, condemning their totalitarian tactics and demanding that the questionaire that was a thinly veiled invasion of personal privacy and totally foreign to the principles of American democracy be sent "back to Mesquite where it came from." Resolutely she urged those who had not filled out the pernicious and degrading document to reject it and not respond.

The extent of the Intelivote's interest in limiting choice was demonstrated in their awarding letter grades to candidates who did not respond. Mayor Harold Patterson received a "C"—and yet had not even seen the questionaire which allegedly contained questions interrogating a candidate's stand on homosexuality, prostitution, gambling and pornography—as well as taxation of church properties. Furthermore, in the manner of the Nazi Party in the early 1930s in Germany, those candidates which Intelivote believed would support their radical right cause were given grades even if they did not respond—such as Place 2 Councilwoman Marti Van Ravenswaay, who received a high grade—or listed as "no response" if the response was not exactly to the political interest of Intelivote.

Disagreement, those who support Intelivote declare, is disruptive and a social evil. Many argue that the division within society, meaning social consciousness towards *weltanschauung* rather than rigid theocratic subjection to the decrees of a demigoguering demigods who pontificate their personal narrow interpretations of ontological and theological writings, comes from public education. Public education, fundamentalists argue, is "godless." The "godlessness" is generated by the "absense of prayer in schools," a policy the Moral Majority and others on the far right wish to undo. If it cannot be done by legislation, and sanctioned by the United States Supreme Court, these totalitarians propose to do away with public education altogether and force religious education on everyone, identical to the atrocity experienced in Iran under its senior ayatollah.[1] That this is the goal of the radical right and strict fundamentalists who openly denounce the evolution of democracy and freedom in America, can be read in the statement of archconservative, Moral Majority, Inc. leader Jerry Falwell

---

[1] See my *Islam & Woman* (Dallas: Monument Press, 1985).

wno preyed: "I hope I live to see the day when, as in the early days of our country, we won't have any public schools. The churches will have taken them over again, and Christians will be running them."[2]

The current trend towards the lack of charity, the open bigotry and unprecedented salvoed sermons of hate and intolerance from the pastors pulpits in Mesquite and throughout Texas is in direct response and laudation of the articulate conservatives rapidly taking over America, dividing North and South more sharply than had ever been experienced—more completely than the Civil War or the issue of race following the Civil War. Rejecting Christ's injunction that "he who takes the sword shall perish by the sword," the New Right, led by Jerry Falwell, pushes for an increased militarization of America under the feigned argument that there is a need for a "stronger national defense"—the word "defense" being bastardized from its original meaning, and clothed in the tyranny of reality being an offensive war.

Well-organized, highly motivated, and well-financed, these new tyrants in America reject civil rights and women's rights in pursuit of the psuedo-purity of the Holiness Code. Censorship is the primary tool of Tomorrow's Tyrants, who demand a limitation on First Amendment rights in religious convocations—especially true within the Southern Baptist Convention, of which Jerry Falwell and the greatest number of the Moral Ma-

---

[2] Judi Lawson Wallace, "What kids read — who decides?" *Ms* magazine (April 1985) p. 21.

jority come from and give their allegiance.

The Southern Baptist Convention's rush to end the separation of church and state is unique in history. Traditionally the Baptists have been opposed to any union or linking between church and state. But under the control of the far right, led by Jerry Falwell and SBC President Charles Stanley, the Southern Baptists recruit for "correct thinking, correct praying, correct believing, born-again Christians" to carry their blood stained banners past the hollowed out shells of bombed abortion clinics, past gnarled trees from which black men have been mercilessly hung, away from the gay ghettos where human beings are economically herded so as to make way for the advance of the Chosen People who fill their church pews and give a minimum tithe of ten percent of their income.

Rejecting the first clause of the one sentence of the First Amendment, which reads: "Congress shall make no law respecting an establishment of religion," but capitalizing on the second clause, which reads: "or prohibiting the free exercise thereof" the radical Right, the Moral Majority, and basic fundamentalists such as Mesquites' intolerant ministers, demand an end to secularism and the estrangement between faith and government.

The absurd lengths some Texas clerics go to deny individuals personal freedoms and rights is best demonstrated in the preachifications of Dr. Richard Land of First Baptist Church in Dallas. Opposed to the ordination of women, derisively calling ordained women "preacherettes" and "pastorettes," this collared cleric calls on Judeo-Christian scriptures to support his stand. Using mock humor, Land questions how a woman could be a "minister of the gospel" when the Book of Timothy requires bishops "to have but one wife." Land refuses to address the actual issue—that the injunction is for bishops, and may be an allegorical statement—inasmuch as the Greek word for minister is deacon, and in the writing of the New Testament a deacon can be of either gender—especially since women were the priests in at least the churches at Rome. This was the celebrated cause of Cliff Temple Baptist Church which refused to renominate Jerry Gilmore of Dallas to another term as a director of the Southern Baptist Convention's Home Mission Board—a post he has held since 1979—a term during which he served as chairperson.

The injustice of the Southern Baptist Convention's bloodless and unconsciousable coup against Attorney Gilmore was even more unfair inasmuch as its decision was based solely on Gilmore's wife having been ordained a minister in the Baptist Church—an ordination accepted by Cliff Temple. He was the only one of 134 demoninational trustees and directors eligible for renomination who was rejected, even though he was acknowledged by Bob Eklund of Dallas, chairperson of the committee, to be an "outstanding layman at Cliff Temple."

The Southern Baptist Convention claims that it is a coalition of autonomous churches with each congregation free to make its own decisions—which Cliff Temple did in 1977, when it approved the ordination of Martha Gilmore. As the situation became increasingly more volatile Ms. Gilmore transferred her membership and ordination to the United Methodist Church, which so enraged Russell Kaemmerling, the radically ultraconservative editor of the Dallas-based fundamentalist publication *Southern Baptist Advocate* that he depreciatorially demanded Gilmore's resignation as director of the Home Mission Board.

Helleborinically harping on his concept of what the bible allegedly declares, Kaemmerling sluggishly spat, "Men whose wives are ordained is an expression of a man's place in the home. Men [allegedly, according to fundamental Southern Baptists] have a special calling as head of the household, and wives should [sic] acquiesce." The total ignorance of scripture as demonstrated in Kaemmerling's crass comment was given less plausibility but additional strength when Taft, California Southern Baptist minister A.C. Holbrook brought the issue of Gilmore's wife's actions up at committee boards when two other committee members from Texas (Eklund and W.O. Watts, a layman from Woodboro) were renominated. His rationale for degrading Gilmore was so that by doing so there would be less trouble on the floor of the Southern Baptist Convention's meeting in Dallas, declaring, "I thought we should come into Dallas with as clean a report as possible—one that would cause as little controversy as possible. There are people who are not going to accept his wife."

The unChristian attitude of Holbrook and Kaemmerling was met with shock by the pastor of Cliff Temple Baptist Church, Rev. Dan Griffin. Appalled by the committee's decision, Griffin lamented, "I deplore the myopia of the fundamentalist-dominated committee. They don't want to know what kind of job he's been doing. He has been praised repeatedly for his even handling of controversial issues on the Home Mission Board." But Gilmore's intense personal faith, selfless ministry to others, and astute ability to handle affairs of the mission mean nothing to the radical right lunatic fringe in control of the Southern Baptist Convention who are determined, like Jerry Falwell, to enchain the mind, harness the heart, and destroy the liberties of those who disagree with their liberty-limiting capricious ukases that are put forth more zealously than that of the Sanhedrin that demanded the life of Stephen and the early Jewish Christians.

The problem in the Gilmore issue is that the Southern Baptist Convention has been over ridden by a tyrannical political network of radical reactionary fundamentalists, led by Falwell, Schlafly, and Atlanta, Georgia Southern Baptist President Charles Stanley who have openly conspired to seize control of the Convention through the machiavellian manipulation of its boards and threatening to escrow cooperative program funding, limit individual human freedom, and prohibit women from exercising their rights as spokespersons of their faith—a tradition as old as Christianity when, in its beginning, women were not only priests but bishops. The radical right of the Southern Baptist Convention has overtly distorted the Christian writings of the past to preach their message of hate, bigotry and intolerance, and use it to whip those who disagree into a mutant state of acceptance and blind obedience. Seldom before has such authoritarianism prevailed within the Southern Baptist Community of Texas, now being exposed in the living martyrdom of Deacon Jerry Gilmore of Cliff Temple Baptist Church, who has been one of the most zealous and strong witnesses to his faith and denomination.

To achieve total control over the minds of America's youth, to stifle any dissent, to propagate continuing escalation of hate and bigotry, the radical Right's most vitriolic viper, Phyllis Schlafly, denounces the freedom to read, the freedom to think, the freedom to decide for oneself the causeway, the destiny, the reality of the individual lifestyle. In *Child Abuse in the Classroom*, which Schlafly is the editor of, urging parents to resist curricula that "blur traditional concepts of gender identity and accept the radical notion of a gender free society in which there are no différences in attitudes and occupations between men and women." Arguing that women *by nature* are inferior to men in strength, intelligence and ability, and that the "rightful" place for women to be is in total subjection to men, she tells housewives to find joy in living in waiting for "their man to come home" so that they can greet this "man" at the door, dressed neatly, with a dinner waiting that will please *him*, and the children either safely in bed or quietly waiting in attendance upon their father's every wish. Her work, like other books she has written, urges America to return to the dark ages of despotic empires that survived by sucking out the life blood of its citizens who were more victims than equal participants. Schalfly's argument, like those of Mesquite's menancing ministers, is that peace comes with lines of demarcation drawn between the sexes, where "equal pay for equal work" is blasphemy, since it takes "femininity away from womanhood."

To this end the move of the radical right is to

censor those books which do not have the same philosophy as they preach. Thus Marlo Thomas' *Free to Be ... You and Me* is condemned as "gender confusion," J.D. Salinger's *The Catcher in the Rye*, is reviewed as "obscene," and Aldous Huxley's *Brave New World* is blasted as "communist propaganda." *The Diary of Anne Frank* is referred to as "subversive" and "a defense of Jewry," while John Steinbeck's *The Grapes of Wrath* is rejected on the grounds that it "gives a bad impression of American business*men*" (my italics), and "presents America in a disfavorable light," for "although the depression was a sad day, it wasn't really that bad." History is to be rewritten where the tale is to be told that everything in America is wonderful, glorious, peaceful,, charitable, prosperous, and other assorted lies. Tragedies that America went through, ranging from the concentration camps that were strung across America during World War II incarcerating native-born Orientals, to the Politics of Fear launched by the demigogue Senator from Wisconsin Joseph McCarthy, to the illegal affront to justice and contempt for the American people by President Richard Nixon, are to be either erased or rewritten to read as if they were benefits for the American people.

This take over of politics is especially threatening in Texas, in the wake of the Sermons of Hate slithering from the pulpits of those who assume the positions of being vicars of God. Among the high priests of this new cult of prejudice is one who defiles the robes of a Roman Catholic prelate. Perniciously he rejects the established canon commission to "minister to the needs of all people," standing for them as an advocate against tyranny, oppression, subjection, and tyranny. Instead he regally rejects his obligations as a pastor and comes out against the very people he is to protect and succor. Bishop John Morkovsky of the diocese of Houston stands, linked philosophically with the Ku Klux Klan and similar bigots, against human rights, freedom of choice and expression.

Bastardizing the Christian Gospel, transmorgifying it from being the "good news of liberation," this pernicious parasitic prelate pounces prattling pontifications pushing human freedoms into the nadir of chaos, while other members of the radical right glory in limiting liberties: denying equal employment opportunity, fair housing guarantees, protection under the law, freedom to read, write, speak and act and live according to personal preferences, proclivities and philosophies.

There has never been a viper more venomously vicious than bishop Thomas Tschoepe of the Dallas Catholic Diocese, who has committed his diocese to support all terrorist actions against women who would exercise their constitutional freedom of choice. Draconically declaring to the Dallas *Times Herald* (13 May 1985), that he endorsed the breaking of secular laws, and promising support to physically restraining women who enter clinics to secure a safe and legal abortion, this calloused cleric has come out on the side of those who would subvert the principles America was founded on and give credence to the tyrants of tomorrow who would have a totalitarian state where only one way was acceptable—their way, without choice, freedom or liberty.

Daily the Catholic church loses adherents who can no longer tolerate the reproachable lack of democracy within the organization, which by its stand against human freedom, has pulled away from the teachings of Jesus to laud the prissy pronouncements of misogynistic males who enthrone their base chauvinism in the church's doctrines. Tschoepe is among the worse offenders who go against human dignity and attempt to ensnare and strangle free thought and self-determination. Yet women fight this tyranny. Women will see the victory!

With the rise of terrorism in Texas, Representative Ralph Wallace, an insensitive racist who draconically declares in ignorance of fact "I can assure you that every black man in Houston carries a gun," has moved in the Texas legislature to make terrorism, violence, bloodshed and murder more easy and regular. Interested in returning to the lawlessness of the wild, wild west, Ralph Wallace recited federal crime statistics as if they were an unimpeachable, infallible litany detailing the need of "true Americans" to bear arms—a "fact"—or way of life— he believes is already taken up by black Americans, lamenting "It's only us stupid whites that [are] sitting over here, we're the ones that aren't carrying a gun."

At no time in his plaintive plaintiff pleading did lawmaker Wallace qualify his statement. At no time did lawmaker Wallace suggest that the possession of a firearm should be legal for a person to own to protect himself. Instead, as if he were jury, judge, and executioner, Ralph Wallace demanded that "us stupid whites" carry a

Ralph Wallace

gun—implying that the carnaged history of the wild west be reintroduced, restored, and reinvigorated—that caucasian citizens strap a gun on to their erson, appear in public bearing firearms, and take the law into their own hands—which might be something to consider in Houston where frequently the police are more dangerous than the criminals.

Ralph Wallace's lust for the lore of the old west appeared in a bill, which he firmed on Monday, 13 May 1985, legislating any Texas citizen to apply for a permit to carry a *concealed* handgun, with the provisos that the gunslinger would have had no prior felony conviction, no pending felony indictments, and a certification from a doctor that "he" is mentally competent. Fortunately the committee of the House took no immediate action on Wallace's eighteenth century sentiment. Some legislators greeted it with open skepticism, even in the face of rising support for such an invitation to lawlessness, crime and capital assaults came from the Texas State Rifle Association.

Passage of such a measure into law would not only encourage greater gun proliferation and use in Texas, but make the streets unsafe, give support to religious fanatics who would pump additional bullets into the homes of physicians and nurses who assist a woman who had made a choice over her own body and the removal of any unwanted group of cells, as well as threaten pro-choice advocates who support the First Amendment. Boot Hill would become more popular than the pool room, the church, or the neighbor's bedroom where more is discussed than politics in some cases.

On Wednesday, 15 May 1985, the Texas House committee moved the Wallace bill to increase crimes of robbery, murder, and violence, in a lopsided vote of 7-1 to permit all Texas citizens to carry a *concealed* handgun on the streets of the state. The days of the Old West are being revived, to the open concern of Abileen Democrat Gary Thompson, the lone objector who voted against the resolution in the Texas House State Affairs Committee.

On Wednesday, 22 May 1985, Texas legalized the potential for great bodily harm and the loss of life when the Texas Senate gave final approval to a measure introduced by Republican Senator J.E. Brown of Lake Jackson to prohibit cities from banning handguns. Returning to the spirit of the old west and lawlessness, the Texas Senate, following the interests of Brown, legislated individual opportunities to assume the position of judge, jury and executioner without need to turn to normal channels. The availability of firearms in Texas has always been easy; now there are no safeguards to protect the commonweal as each individual is not only overtly allowed to possess any and all guns desired, but covertly invited to carry concealed weapons and use them at will regardless of provocation or lack their of. J.E. Brown has, in truth, not only legalized but encouraged organized crime and a return to they days of Bonnie and Clyde and lawlessness where guns were more powerful than reason or law. As crime increases and murders multiply in response to the Brown measure, Texas will applaud the farsighted concern for public safety exercised by the rational and compassionate Senator Brown.

Sid Fitzwater

The Old Guard:
Democrat and Republican
and
Yuppie Justice

Texas conservativism exceeds even the tyranny of corruption of Texas politics in its abuse of juridical powers and the mastication of justice. Sid Fitzwater of Dallas embodies everything that is bad in Texas justice.

Following the trend of the young urban profession who thinks only of the self and the self's aggrandizement with no thought of the needs of others, Sid Fitzwater, at age 31, became the rising star of the Reagan administration to preach the grotesque gosepl of entrenchment and stagnation of justice in the U.S. district court system—a promise that his political far-right philosophies and interpretations of the laws will last for decades into the future. Fitzwater follows the fault line of the Reagan timetable to undo all of the progressive populist acts of the Roosevelt administration, where individual rights of women, minorities, the oppressed and disenfranchised are sneeringly laughed at and made the butt of the miscarriage of justice so that the elite and wealthy can further limit if not destroy the entire middle class in their crass movement to build a patronic base of despocy in America.

The bitterness that Fitzwater feels towards women, especially, is seen in his constant anti-choice stand, articulating that an non-mature fetus has greater rights than the rights of the mother to whom it is appended. The district court judgeship will mean that not only will abortion rights be severely limited but possibly eliminated in Dallas. With such an impudent judgement a man who is openly hostile to the needs of women in general, all women's rights and state of advancement will come under scorching scrutiny and ultimately the chopping block as their democratic rights are severed and pulverized into dust with the rap of a hardened gavel.

Not only will women's rights suffer under Sid Fitzwater, but the entire progress of basic civil rights be fired upon by a salvo of bitterness and personal bigotry reporting from his bench. Blacks, Mexican-Americans and other hyphenated nationals can only look forward towards an inevitability of social, economic and even political disenfranchisement, restrictions, and limitations, for Fitzwater supports the Reagan philosophy of doing away with many of the Civil Rights Acts Titles on the spurious and illogical grounds that they are too expensive, wasteful, and unnecessary. As Ann Lewis of the Americans for Democratic Action calculated, courts such as that of Fitzwater will reverse past judicial rulings and herald the advent of trouble for generations to come if those generations believe in democracy and equal protection and justice under the law.

Personal judgements, neither based on the written law or on common law, are not new in Texas. Fourth District Justice of the Peace Frank Berry of Dallas County is well known for rendering verdicts based on his own feelings rather than upon any standard of legality, as was dramatically the case in *Mitchell vs. General Homes*. The case is by no means unique. In *Mitchell vs. General Homes*, the plaintiff brought suit against General Homes, seeking $1,000 (the maximum amount which can be sought in Texas in a Small Claims Court) to help defray a quotation of $2,400 presented the plaintiff by a contractor who would repair the cracks which developed in the plaintiff's property. Mitchell alleged that the cracks in his garage floor and around foundation. Under oath Mitchell detailed that he had purchased the home from its original owner who had secured the property by a bill of sale from General Homes. Mitchell stated that he felt that General Homes should honor their original warranty against defective craftpersonship and relay the floor, build a new facade (the current one pulled away from the structure of the dwelling), and render better drainage to the property. Mitchell stated that when he requested these services General Homes responded by detailing that the warranty was not transferable, but they did agree to come out and inspect the property and make a judgement as to what they could do. Several visits were made, allegedly, although Mitchell was not present at the time General Homes personnel arrived on the premises. Concluding his initial comments, Mitchell called upon a companion for his observations—even though the companion was not trained in civil or other engineering sciences.

The companion affirmed the testimony of Mitchell. He, too, detailed the separation of the facade from the structure, the crack in the garage floor, and the standing water around the foundation. Alarmed that General Homes had not made good their warranty, he detailed, he urged Mitchell to seek legal action.

Following the testimony of the Mitchell coterie, General Homes' attorney and key personnel approached Frank Berry's bench. In evidence of their claim that they were not bound by law or warranty to correct any defective work, the attorney introduced the warranty, and had Mitchell read to the court the contents which detailed explicitly that the warranty was not transferrable to a second or additional owners of the original property. The attorney then introduced their key personnel, beginning with the general services manager who testified that he had personally gone to the Mitchell property, inspected the damage, and concluded that General Homes was not at fault. The standing water was a result of an outdoor faucet being left on, the crack, which was viewable from the outside (and, since he did not have access to the interior) of the garage floor, he concluded that it was a result of natural ground swelling and settling, common in Texas. This hypothesis was supported by the General Homes engineer and a representative from the ground surveyors.

For approximately two hours testimony was given. Evidence was presented by both sides: Mitchell offering photographs of the damage, and General Homes presenting warranty contracts, testimony, and other legal manuevers.

Judge Berry asked the plaintiff if he knew that the warranty he was citing was not transferrable. Mitchell confessed that he did, but felt that it *should* be tranferrable in his favor. Berry then posed the question to General Homes as to whether or not they stood behind their product. General Homes' response was that they honored all written warranties, and that they had corrected any defect in any property they built and sold provided that the correction was executed under the provisions of the contract agreed upon and signed by the buyer and seller.

Sluggishly sinking into his leather padded seat, Berry issued his opinion. Berry argued that if *he* bought a house—regardless if it was from the home builder or anyone else—he would expect it to be warranted at least during the first year of his occupancy. Defying and rejecting all rules of jurisprudence, Berry boisterously intoned that he would award judgment to the plaintiff since the existing warranty issued by General Homes did not conform to his personal opinion of what a home builder should do, even though he accepted the fact that the warranty was both legal and valid and had the strength of law on its side.

The *Mitchell vs. General Homes* case was not

atypical. His court room is a circus of personal vendetta against any plaintiff or defendent he takes an instant disliking towards. When a woman appeared in court seeking recourse against a neighbor who was taking her flowers, Berry's response was that "flowers grow naturally and do not recognize ownership." When she broke into tears he threatened her with removal to the state mental institution "as I just can't stand to see a grown woman cry. I'll have none of that in this court."[1]

D magazine (December 1983) made a lengthy presentation of Dallas judges, detailing how some get no respect and others don't deserve it. Frank Berry and Sid Fitzwater, unfortunately, have many colleagues who malfunction as they do.

The extent of the venality of Texas justice was dramatically illustrated on Thursday, 7 March 1985, when Dallas County Criminal Judge Harold Entz admitted he disregarded the law by ignoring an allegation of serious bodily injury against Martin Rivera of Garland who was involved in an accident. Entz found Rivera guilty of a lesser charge of driving while intoxicated. Entz's confession came as a result of a hearing to determined if he should

---

[1] In 1979, concerning *Ide vs. Bjornlin*, where the plaintiffs testified that the defendents had taken house fixtures from plaintiffs' residence, and had occupied the same premises for more than two months past closing and notice to move (during which time plaintiffs were liable for all utilities and other costs incurred by the property being occupied by the defendents), Berry, in a closed session, declared that he would have taken even the light bulbs if he had sold the house and ruled in favor of the defendemts pm the grounds that the Bjornlins were being required to move during a spring shower which inconvenienced Mrs. Bjornlin. This ruling was issued in spite of the record that the Bjornlins testified that they had stayed in the house against the expressed wishes of the new owners, used utilities and other items at the cost of the plaintiffs, and had deliberately taken the fixtures which had not been exempted in the bill of sale.

disqualify himself from further involvement in the case which was being tried by the District Attorney's office.

His court room policies which have been criticized for a number of years, came under sharp attack following the Rivera incident. The attack became even more razor fine when Entz admitted he had also disregarded a probable cause affidavit that alleged that several passengers riding in the car that was struck by Rivera's truck had suffered serious and possibly fatal injuries in the accident. Entz said he ignored the affidavit when Rivera told him that there had been no injuries, and reasoned, from that testimony, that the affidavits contained possible erroneous information. When confronted with additional evidence of his misjudgement, Entz declared that Rivera was at fault for giving him "perjurous testimony," and that he was not responsible since he had based his decision upon Rivera's presentation.

Rejection of the principles on which America was founded, and defiance of Supreme Court rulings refining the United States Constitution is not a monopoly of Dallas County judges. Machinations to overturn significant civil liberties judgments and rule against human rights appears throughout Texas in many courts, but no where more machiavellianly than in the Houston court of Federal U.S. District Judge Norman Black, who is making a one person crusade against the basic principle of separation between church and state.

Caving in to the demands of Tony Amidei, a senior at Westchester High School in the Spring Branch School District, Judge Black has ruled that the school must make taxpayer space in the school open for sectarian and dogmatic purposes of a single faith in preference over other faiths. Black has accepted the partisan issues presented in the Amidei petition to allow "a small group of students who has a common interest in Christianity and the life and teachings of Jesus Christ to meet once a week for one hour to discuss common experiences." No mention was made of the other students' rights to meet to discuss the preachings and life of other gods or prophets.

Clearing and consciously rejecting the Founding Father's warning to keep church and state separate lest all personal freedoms evaporate in the on-coming fires of religious persecution by one sect over other sects and non-believers, Judge Black capriciously ruled that Amidei and his compatriots could use taxpayer facilities for personal interests even if the taxpayers were not of like mind or intent. Overriding the protection of the many for the enjoyment of a few, Black gave his blessing to a clearly unConstitutional law originally passed by Congress in 1984—a ruling that District Superintendent Henry Wheeler has not interest enough in challenging or willingness to denounce as a flagrant violation of civil liberties in America.

Texas taxpaying citizens are Christian, Jew, Moslem, Buddhist, atheist, Hindu, and a plethora of other denominations, cults, faiths, metaphysical affirmations, and confessions. Each individual, regardless of religious or theosophic belief or disbelief is guaranteed the freedom to belief or not to believe in a deity or

special interest not only in the Constitution of the United States but in the Texas Constitution. Furthermore, all citizens of Texas and of the United States are guaranteed a division and a separation of church and state, and that not only will the churches of the nation be separated from interfering with the progress of the state, but forbidden to jeopardize one religion or lack of religion for the sake, propagandization and proselytization of a religion over another or against the lack thereof. Yet Tony Amidei, like diphosgenic dictator from

Tony Amidei
Religion enthroned in the Public Classroom
The end to the separation of church & state

some backward nation that lives in terror of its more articulate spokespeople has taken it upon himself for his own selfish interests to tear assunder the principle of freedom of, for, and from religion and end the separation between church and state by demanding that all taxpayers in Houston afford him the opportunity and privilege of using their money and their facilities to further his own philosophic, theologic, and personal interests in testifying to that faith he and a small handfull of like-minded individuals affirm.

On 26 April 1985, the principles the Founder Fathers of America cherished so dearly as to risk their property, fortunes, and lives in declaring in the Declaration of Independence and later in the Constitution of the United States of America, that *all* men—not just a few radicals—were to be free, to puruse and pursue happiness in each individual's own way, were blown away after their sacred character was smashed by the ghoulish gavel of U.S. District Judge Norman Black who paved the way for religious totalitarianism and the take over of the public school system in Houston. Like a tax collector or money changer in the temple, Tony Amidei prissly presided over a clinquant coterie of co-conspirators who made a mockery out of religion and the injunction of their deity who declared around two thousand years ago, "If you pray, do so in secret," admonishing against "praying in public like pharisees and other hypocrits" who misuse religious expression to be seen by others.

The problem is simple. Tony Amidei is using a secular classroom funded and supported by taxpayers of various ideologies for to augment, further, proselytize, disseminate, propagandize his personal religious beliefs. This is in direct violation of the Constitutional guarantee of the separation of church and state.

Eignteen year old Winchester senior Tony Amidei declared that the laws which had stopped his *public* profession of faith were the work of "Satan," justifying his push based on Psalm 37 which reads "The Lord sustains the righteous," impishly implying his self-righteousness and the irreligiosity of others, while he sat enthroned in a public room catering to a private affair at taxpayers expense. Deliberately and consciously violating the democratic principles of separation of church and state, this demigogue predicts that his affront will be pushed by tyrants throughout other school districts in Texas. Selectively principled and voicing a single cult, Amidei has yet to encourage the establishment of a Buddhist Club, Club of Islam, atheist club, or any other expression of individual theological or religious awareness circles.

U.S. District Judge James DeAnda deserves no respect and merits the contempt of all Texans who believe in justice, fairness, and due process. A most contemptible judge who acts capriciously and outside of the law, well known for dismissing cases against police officers of Houston—a law enforcement agency which has become a textbook case of corruption and self-interest greed— James DeAnda has rejected pleas of citizens who have been harassed, abused, and threatened by the police of Houston who are more interested in entrapment of citizens than in protecting citizens of actual crimes—forcing their way into alleged brothals while rape takes place in nearby bushes.

The ignominy of the tyranny of this pernicious jurist appeared in its most grotesque manner when DeAnda dismissed the long-running rape case of Pedro Tijerina IV the first week of May 1985, stating in his order that the "Plaintiff's failure to pursue this action forced this court to conclude that he is lacking in due diligence."—an order which was issued on 22 March 1985. The case involves Harris County Deputy Sheriff W.E. DeLeon who forced Tijerina at the Harris County Criminal Courts building to twice perform oral sodomy on himself in the fall of 1983.

The Tijerina case is not unique. Officer DeLeon has been accused of forcing no less than four other inmates in the County jail to perform oral sodomy on his person. Officer DeLeon continues his coersive sexual rape of male inmates under the guise of transporting them to court, even though he is not the baliff in any of Houston's courts. But acting as a self-appointed bailiff, moving prisoners to the various courtroom from the Harris County Jail around four or five in the morning, DeLeon has had the opportunity to become familiar with Judge DeAnda. DeAnda is not known to forget favors of people who work for him.

The outcome of this case initiated by Tijernia is not unusual, for this insensitive judge is the same abuser of civil liberties who dismissed cases in The Valley earlier when shown video tapes of officers beating up jailed inmates. In these cases the claim was that there was "insufficient evidence" to prosecute.

Bill Ceverha—
Taking Aim at Human Freedom

Evil did not die in the German bunker occupied by Adolf Hilter. Machinations against human dignity did not end with the death of Stalin. Plots to overthrow civil liberties and quash human freedom is not the monopoly of only a few hooded hoodlums parading in white sheets who burn crosses in the yards of Blacks and Jews, calling themselves Christians while appealing only to the most base animalistic and unreasoning instincts of prejudice. For the characteristics of hate and ignorance that the world has shunned for the most part as unbefitting a thinking being who is a member of the mortal race of humankind flourish and flower in the tepid mind and vitriolic verbage that spews from the torrid tyrannical tongue of Texas' most awesome demigogue Republican Bill Ceverha who allegedly represents the interests of the 112th District.

Guided by personal instincts and parochial

politics, this legislator, more than any other law maker—with the possible exceptions of Jan McKenna and Bob McFarland—cruelly campaigns craftily against human beings who he labels as less than dogs. Representing north Dallas, all of Richardson, and a small portion of Garland, Ceverha in 1985 was serving his fifth consecutive term in the state House. Carol Castlebury, Ceverha's administrative aide in Austin, has declared to the press[1] that Ceverha's constituency supports his radical views to limit freedom—especially the rights of homosexuals to

Bill Ceverha

---

[1] Mark Blazek, "Re-Introduction of Sodomy Bill Possible in State L̲ ̲ ̲ ̲ture, but Passage Unlikely," *Texas Star* (25 January 1985) p. 1.

be live and work with dignity in a society where individuals are treated equally and judged only on their ability to produce, their contributions to the commonwealth, and their dedication to the rights and liberties of others. Yet, in the face of this and in strong opposition to the primary guarantees of both the Texas Constitution and the Constitution of the United States of America, Ceverha has come out publically and politically to deny homosexuals equal housing, equal employment opportunities, and equal protection under the law and in the courts.

Castlebury argues that Ceverha is against homosexuals because of the growing fear of AIDS—which in her ignorance she argues is a "gay disease" even though small children, nuns, women, and heterosexuals have contacted the dreaded and deadly disease which took the life of the "Bubble Boy" David of Houston who had been confined since his early days in a plastic environment where sterility was the rule and he was under constant supervision. Betty Naylor, executive director of the Gay Lobby to the Bar Owners Association of Texas, has a different interpretation of Ceverha's irrational homophobia—it is her contention that Ceverha plays on the popular fear of homosexuals in order to further his own political ambitions. These ambitions could lead this calloused crusader against human liberty to the Governor's Mansion, the Senate—and it is rumored—even to the White House where America's most insensitive president who silently backs the murderous atrocities of the Nazi's resides—showing his support by not only planning a visit to a German cemetery where SS (storm troopers) are buried, but by trying to excuse and justify his actions by the lame comment that the men who were inducted into Hitler's Army of the Third Reich were "as much a victim" of Hitler as were the 6 million Jews and countless other opponents of Der Fuehrer who lost their lives in the concentration camps of his empire.

The tragedy of growing homophobia in Texas is the fact that many gays are themselves homophobic. Afraid of their own affectional interests and sexual proclivities, many are "gay" during the earliest part of their youth, and then, to be "socially acceptable," obtain a well-paying job, and conform to the full insanity of yuppie psychology, marry a member of the opposite sex, procreate a child or children, and then long for an intimate relation with members of their own gender. Frequently this longing develops into clandestine meetings in parks, "bookstores" which are adult emporiums for sexually explicit materials or devices, bars, bath houses, or dark alleys. Other homosexuals who are afraid to be themselves, have married and sired children, longing to be free of the encumberances they have placed upon themselves, even solicit relationships or sex in popular magazines as *The Dallas Observer*, the *Advocate*, or *This Week In Texas,* or in newsheets such as *The Fort Worth Star*, the *Dallas Voice*, San Antonio *Post*, or any other of the numerous local papers.

Gays have become their own worse enemy. Not only do they refuse to patronize their own stores (with the exception of the bars and bath), they campaign for and vote for distinctly and sharply anti-gay candidates, as occurred in the 1984 election when gays organized a "Gays for Gramm" campaign to elect rigidly anti-gay Phil Gramm to the United States Senate. The Gay Republican Caucus has twice endorsed Ronald Reagan for president, eventhough their candidate has openly stated that he would never approve of any legislation guaranteeing gays basic civil rights or legal protection from discrimination; and the Gay Conservative Caucus has endorsed George Strake's move to limit gay freedom, overlooking Strake's absolutely anti-gay comments, such as blasting "dykes on bikes" during the 1984 GOP Convention in Dallas.

Eager to be accepted as "one of the good ol' boys," gays rallied against the Houston Referendum to prohibit job discrimination, and voted to limit their own rights in job quests, securement, and protection. Numerous gays have even come out against Mayor Whitmore of Houston, supporting anti-gay candidates who seek to take her job.

Ceverha is not the only outspoken homophobe in Texas who is attempting to control human sexuality, for he is joined in spirit and ambition by rank San Antonio City Councilwoman Maria Berriozabal who made headlines the second week of May 1985 for her irrational stand to close a gay bar as a pilot to her Neronian goal of "cleaning up the city". As if she were John Calvin piling faggots of wood around a heap of human-created material goods, wooing the demons of hell in an effort to sustain her blind lust for power in playing god, City Councilwoman Maria Berriozabal wrung her hands like Pilot and piously declared that she would "clean up the area surround the 200 block of Broadway."

Not only does this saccharin salicylistic pseudo-savior sanctimoniously sing pslams of damnation and purgation on the homosexual bars of San Antonio—establishments she has never visited and thus is totally ignorant of—but she spews seeds of saliferous hatred into the sores of bristling insanity by pledging her efforts to close down all downtown bars—which she must, if she is not to expose her pettiness of being against human rights, include not only gay bars—which, logically, must include the River Walk clubs and the posh San Antonio hotel bars. Lacking any admissable proof, be it photographs or eye witnesses, Berriozabal damns a group of people on the alleged complaint that there are "men naked in front of business establishments during the day" along the Broadway strip in an effort to force the San Antonio police to increase their patrols.[2] No naked men have been found—except in venomous lamentations liquifying from the dark side of Berriozabal's mind, flowing out into passionate denunciations of freedom of congregation, selection, and speech. Hitler had aimed at purifying the German race in the first half of the twentieth century by limiting who could meet where, what could be said or seen, and under what circumstances interactions could take place, putting to death millions of innocent peo-

---

[2] "City Councilwoman Want to Close Gay Bars," *This Week in Texas* (17-23 May 1985) p. 15.

ple because they did not share his values, nor were they "acceptable individuals" who met his rigid and disabling criteria on the basis of race, religion, sex, sexual preference, politics, and the like. Berriozabal now comes to the pages of history with an identical message, for she does not believe that individuals have rights of action or choice in matters that do not conform to her puritanical standards and hegemonic interests.

This attempt at mind control and action orientation, however goes beyond sexual orientation. It spills over into the ocean of other freedoms which Berriozabal would control, and Ceverha diligently debates in Austin. Chief among these is the right to believe in a god or gods, or not believe in anything at all. Ceverha heads the list of tyrants who would require that all office holders affirm the existence of a deity, even if the elected official does not chose to believe in anything other than the dignity and rights of the individual.

The problem of Bill Ceverha of Richardson is that he is attempting to make his voice supreme and the law of the land—going beyond statutes established by the Texas legislature and sanctioned by time. This is most graphically seen in his undemocratic move to strip the Office of the Attorney General of its power to settle federal law suits by having them determined and settled by non-elected state agency heads. This, in effect, would make the Office of the Attorney General ineffective and unnecessary, to the detriment of Texas.

Partisan politics at its very worse, Ceverha's bill introduced in May 1985 is a petty reaction against

Jim Mattox who settled two federal lawsuits when he agreed to allow women the right to participate in the originally sexist all-male Texas A&M band, and, second, when he ruled that state office holders did not have to believe in a god. Refusing to play politics, keeping the freedom of the people of Texas in mind, Jim Mattox noted that both efforts to limit choice and opportunity were unconstitutional and guaranteed that he would rule that judgement if it came to a test of strength.

The misogynistic chauvinism of Bill Ceverha, traditionally at a bargain-basement level, filtered obscenities obnoxious to thinking human beings when he rallied in favor of sex discrimination against women, citing the "history" of the Aggie band being "exclusively male"—interesting and unique inasmuch as Ceverha has historically come out against what he alleges is exclusively male, that being homosexuality. Does Ceverha believe that every male member of the Texas A&M band is heterosexual, or that playing an instrument to root the Aggies on makes the musician heterosexual? Or does he believe that women are not only incompetent to play in an Aggie band or that by playing in the Aggie band they are going to "tempt" the male players as allegedly Eve tempted the mythical Adam?

Then, too, is Ceverha's highhanded totalitarian concept of civic consciousness. Do atheists really wish the state evil? Are people who do not believe in a god "bad citizens" or unqualified to speak for others? What does a person's individual religious affirmation in any deity have to do with their ability to function in politics, business, society, the home, or any other situation? Religious freedom—freedom to chose religion and freedom to reject the same (or remain indifferent to it) was not only the guiding principles of the writers of the Constitution but the very heart of the Constitution—especially when one notes that few of the Founding Fathers of American history had any strong religious interests or ties to any denomination or cult. In truth it appears that Ceverha is pushing "Christianity" as being synonymous to "acknowledge[ing] the presence of a Supreme Being," for by doing so the various religions which do not affirm the eternality of the soul or the existence of a Supreme Being would not qualify by his capricious and irrational standard.

In a rare burst of courage the editors of *Texas Monthly* (July 1985, pp. 114-124) published a strong, stunningly insightful and conscientiously thought-through article on the ten best and ten worse legislators. At the bottom of the legislative quagmire of incompetence and petty vindictiveness the editors have sagely sifted through the cesspool record of Richardson's regressive radical right Senator Ceverha, and objectively offered their readers not only a truly splendid review, but a cogent analysis of one of Texas' least effective and most abrasive legislators. Ceverha's prime concern is weasling into private individual's basic civil liberties to bloat them beyond personal recognition until they resemble his tympanic twitches pushed past reason to become the law of Texas is the focus of this classic article. It is presented in a most clinically conscientious and scholarly manner. No machination of the reactionary Richardson legislator is left covered, unexplored, or free from careful dissection. The rich patina of the editor's work exposes the tarnished tricks of Ceverha whose goals all seem to lead to personal aggrandizement, the denigration of those who disagree with him, and the end of basic civil rights by those he wishes to disenfranchise.

Texas Monthly has carved up the cornucopia of legislative corruption seen in the do-nothingness of several legislators, as well as the egocentricism of others. Ceverha has nearly everyone beat in the area of ineptness and pseudorepresentation. The only other legislator who comes close to the totalitarian threats of Ceverha, *Texas Monthly* points out, is Arlington's Senator Jan McKenna, who has become the greatest and most outspoken foe of Texas women, blasting the freedom of choice, and working to limit if not destroy the freedom to read and know as currently guaranteed in the United States Constitution.

INDEX

abortion.........3, 87-103
..................141
abused children.26, 136-37
Acquired Immuned Deficiency Syndrome (AIDS).81, 157
Advocacy, Inc..........19
agrieconomics......62-66
American Agricultural Movement........57-59
Americans for Democratic Action.............142
American Nazi Party101-107
Amidei, Tony and the end of separation of church and state.......146-155
Arlington, TX..7-16, 128-29
Armey of God...89-90, 100
Armey, Richard...20, 44-55
..................77
  and civil rights....46-47
  on farmers..48-49, 63, 65
  on federal budget..46-47
  on hunger........45-49
  on nuclear energy.50-51
  on sex discrimination.47
  on small business....48
  on wages.........49-50
  on war......46-48, 51-52
  on wealth...........50
  on women..........50
Arnett, TX..........26-27
Austin Middle School in Garland, TX.......41-43

Barnes, Ken...........43
Barney, Jan..........128
Beale, Deanna.........43

Beatty, Cummins......88
Bender. Art............10
Bentsen, Sen. Lloyd...118
Barry, Judge Frank.142-45
bible and tyranny.......8
Bielss, Bradley James108-09
Black, Judge Norman146-155
  on ending separation of church and state..146
..............153-155
Blake, William.........32
Blanton, Bill............8
Boatright, Henry.......28
Bolz, Jeff.............84
Bradley, Don.......125-26
Bruner, Gary..........13
Bruni, Eileen..........25
Bush, George W. (Sr.)..117
Bush, George W. (Jr.)..117
Bushy, Mamie.........33

censorship......5-8, 26-40
Ceverha, Bill.......155-65
Cheaney, Sheila.....94-95
choice as a right...3, 89-90
Christianity as disguise.74
church and state issue144-55
civil rights of minorities.17
....18-26, 141-42, 153-60
Clark, Doug..........107
Cleburn, TX.........17-23
Cliff Temple Baptist Church controversy132-35
Crowder, Coach James109
..................110
Culver, Jimmy......92-93
Curry, Peter Michael100-101

Curtis, James 35, 36, 87, 101

Dallas County Commissioners on the mentally retarded 24
Dickens, Charles *A Christmas Carol*.............. 45
Dix, Dorothea......... 20
Doggett, Sen. Lloyd... 118
drug abuse........... 68

education
    at home............ 4-5
    religious......... 4, 130
Eklund, Bob.......... 133
Entz, Harold....... 145-46
Euless, TX.......... 28-32

Falwell, Jerry and terrorism in Texas.... 99, 100, 101
.... 107, 129, 131, 134

Farm Credit System.. 64-65
farm foreclosures... 64, 67
.... 72, 76
farmers....... 56-73, 80-81
    mental health of... 60-61
    poverty of........ 59-61
    suicides of....... 59-60
First Amendment to the U.S. Constitution, limitations placed on it....... 13-16
.... 28-40, 101
Fitzwater, Judge Sid 139-142
free market........... 62
    see also Armey, Richard
Forest Park (Arlington). 106
Forisha, Bill........... 38
Fort Worth, TX and terrorism............. 105-115
Fridrich, Pam....... 94-95
Frischman, Marvin..... 98

Galveston, TX......... 21
Garland, TX......... 41-43
Garland, Marion..... 58-59
Glickman, Dan......... 57
Gilmore, Jerry..... 132-135
Gilmore, Rev. Martha.. 133
Goebbels, Joseph Paul 107
Goldsby, Matthew (terrorist) . 1 0 0
Gramm, Sen. Phil... 20, 58
.... 59, 63, 65, 76-77
Gray, Susan........ 14, 15
Griffin, Dan.......... 134
Groves, Ken... 8, 11-12, 13
guns, ownership of 109-115

Hall, Ralph........... 53
Hall, Sam............. 53
Hance, Kent...... 116-121
handicapped people.... 79
    see also mentally handicapped
Hannah, Jan.......... 18
Harkin, Sen. Tom...... 57
Hart, Jim............. 1-2
Hayes, Kaye.......... 101
Heckler, Margaret... 77, 80
Heiland, Rich...... 10-11n
Helms, Sen. Jesse... 57-58
Hightower, Jim (Texas Agricultural Commissioner) on farmers....... 57-58
Hillside Home...... 24-25
Hitler, Adolf . 3, 91, 105, 155
Holbrook, A.C......... 134
homosexuality. 7-8, 79, 106
.... 155-160
Humphrey, Sen. Gordon 102

Intelivote......... 123-129
Irving, TX and the mentally ill 23-24

justice for sale........41

Kaemmerling, Russell and
 religious intollerance133
134
King, Carl.............60
Kirkpatrick, Jeane......63
Ku Klux Klan..........121
Kubiak, L.B.........93-95

LaMarche, Gara.......91
Lancaster, TX.........21
Land, Richard........132
Leath, Marvin.......53-54
Leedom, John......20, 45
Legal Services Corp.....83
Legion of Doom...105-115
Leland, Mickey........45
Lesley, Freddy.........59
Lewis, Ann...........142
Lipscomb, Wyatt W.111124
Luna, Earl.............22
lynchings..............2
Lynn, Dottie.....12, 13, 14

Mattox, Jim...........42
Mauzy, Oscar..........91
McDonald Corp........68
McFarland, Bob
 of Arlington......32, 34
 .....38, 39, 91-92, 93, 95
 of Euless.........30-32
McKenna, Jan........1-6
 .....32, 34, 38, 93, 95, 96
Medicaid..........24, 76
mentally handicapped
 social treatment of...17
18-26
Mesquite, TX....89-93, 124
Meyer, Edwin C......97-98

*Mitchell vs. General
 Homes*........142!143
Military spending......84
Monaghan, T. Patrick..100
Mondale, Walter.......76
Moral Majority, Inc.....117
 ....123, 129-131
Morrison, Cecil........59
Morkovsky, John
 (Houston bishop)...138

NAACP...............42
Nathanson, Bernard.95-96
National Organization for
 Women *see* NOW
Naylor, Betty..........157
Nazi Party in U.S...130, 157
 see also Legion of
 Doom
Nedderman, Wendell.32-40
Neo-Nazis in U.S...105-115
Nixon, Richard M......121
North, Beverly.........89
Northrop, Bobbie......18
Norwood, Jim.....7-16, 32
Novotny, Susan.......100
NOW.................89
Nystrom, Brunhilde
 of Mesquite........126
127

Oak Cliff, TX........24-26
O'Laughlin, Miles.....120

Patterson, Harold
 of Arlington.....128-129
Paschall, R.L. High
 School.....105-115, 121
Penthouse......10, 14, 30
Playboy.........10, 14, 30

pornography 5-6,
.... 10, 28, 29, 30
Porter, Robert......... 19
poverty 46-55, 79-80
.... 81-82, 117
see also Armey, Richard
see also Hance, Kent
see also Reagan, Ronald
see also Stockwell, David
see also Gramm, Phil
Price, Bill 88
prostitution 68
Public Broadcasting
cuts in 83-84

racism 41-43
see also Wallace, Ralph
see also Hance, Kent
Randol Mill Park....... 8-9
Rakin, Pasko.......... 97
Reagan, Ronald... 3, 20, 25
..... 56-59, 67, 74, 87, 96
Administration of 222220
... 25, 54, 67, 139, 141-42
Reagonomics 25
religious fanaticism... 123
.... 124-160
Republican Party.... 25
.... 61, 62, 121
Roe vs. Wade....... 89, 90
Roosevelt, Franklin D... 65
Rosenberg, Roger...... 99

Schlafly, Phillys.. 107, 136
Silent Scream 95-103
Schroeder, Pat...... 45-46
7-11 *see* Southland Corp.
Sharp, John........ 91-92
Simmons, James..... 100
Katherine.......... 100
see also terrorism

Southern Baptist
Convention..... 131-135
Southland Corp........ 14
Stanley, Charles...... 131
"Star Wars"........ 44, 59
"states rights"...... 17-26
Stenholm, John........ 53
Stiles, Mark.......... 119
Stockman, David.... 61-63
Strake, George..... 20, 61
Student Loan Assoc.... 83
Sullivan, Greg....... 33-34
see also terrorism

Tate, David C......... 114
taxes.............. 66, 80
terrorism...... 99-115, 138
see also Falwell, Jerry
see also Legion of
Doom
see also Moral Majority
see also Simmons
James
Katherine
see also Tschoepe,
Thomas, bishop
see also Wiggins, Kaye
see also Yuppie
mentality
Texas Growers Assoc... 60
Texas Dept. Health..... 23
theocratic tyranny..... 16
see also Amidei, Tony
Trinity Baptist Church
of Arlington.......... 14
Tschoepe, Thomas
(bishop of Dallas)... 138
see also terrorism
Univesity of Texas
at Arlington *see*
Nedderman, Wendell

UTA Baptist Student
   Union............33-34
   ....35, 38

Vassey, Gen. John.....86
Vaughn, Kenneth....14-15
Voltaire, Jean Marie....32

wages, minimum....66-69
  78
war fever.............86
Watkins, Admiral James
   and war............86
Watts, W.O...........134
West Central Texas
   Council of Governments
  60
White, Gov. Mark..118, 157

Whitehead, Bob......113
Whitley, G.I............27
Wiggins, Kaye........100
   see also terrorism
Wilson, Fridrich Meg...91
women and oppression
   ....79, 80, 102
Women's Clinic of
   Mesquite.........87-89

youth wages........66-69
Yuppie mentality.......19
   ....69, 105, 139-159
   see also Legion of
   Doom
   see also terrorism

Zimmerman, Louis.....22